CONTENTS

THE COSMIC FLOW

THE COSMIC FLOW

MANDALAS, MEDITATIONS, AND KINDNESS

JUAN FELIPE HERRERA

NOEMI

Published by Noemi Press, Inc. A Nonprofit Literary Organization. www.noemipress.org

Cover & Book Design by co•im•press

ISBN: 978-1-955992-56-5

RUMI(NATIONS) FROM INSIDE THE MANDALA

Everything is a circle.

All is in constant motion and in constant interaction, interpenetration, and becoming.

The mandala taps and connects, communicates with the infinite,
the cosmos — maybe because everyone of us is an intimate atomic
structure and body constantly and deeply in contact with the spheres
of all life, earth, sky, and space.

Ask a neutrino and a photon.

It is good to open new roads and lines and new relationships and find
truths once buried and hidden.

Be in the flow with
all beings here and across the cosmos.

Life is interplanetary, otherwise we
would not exist.

+

500 days of spontaneity,
an automatic movement
of the hand and mind—a circular leaf
documents COVID-19, Black Lives Matter, Ukraine,
and all the fractures.

+

How great it is to center our lives, our poetry, our seeing mind and hands in the circle of humanity, kindness, and cosmos. Perhaps it is the answer, the solution to our present state of destruction in the world and self-annihilation in our own nation—so many wars and tidal waves of violence, genocide, racism, re-segregation, the erosion of values and harmony.

We must re-enter our inner sources of compassion and kindness.

We can draw and contemplate these quandaries through a mandala poetics.

It is possible.

+

The mandala of the universe is always in rotation, waiting
for you to write upon it and from its center
in order to inscribe your life words and inner-spark
phrases unleashed. Loosen the inner-self breath
of kindness across the whirling sectors
of the mind, the cosmos —for the people.

MEDITATION I
WE

We act we push the cosmos

w/kindness
we take a step
true life we continue
what is the ultimate reality
this wheel of all things
w/o knowing it

una canción
un limón
una guitarra
unas maracas
una vida
un danzón
the monument comes down
the streets are painted
is it angelic

we forget the light
is written on our face
illusion perceptions
nothingness

the waters again
again
the piercing of the earth
the neutrinos
heat the volcanic shafts
long ago in the ocean
beginnings

here
we
are
here we enter we thread
into earth
time wheel
life

do not fret
flowers & poems we offer
every moment
we say
thank you every moment
we celebrate
every second
the interplanetary rotation
into ourselves

unity
star shapes
molecules all molecules

all is shifting

SEE
HE DAY
WE
9/16/20

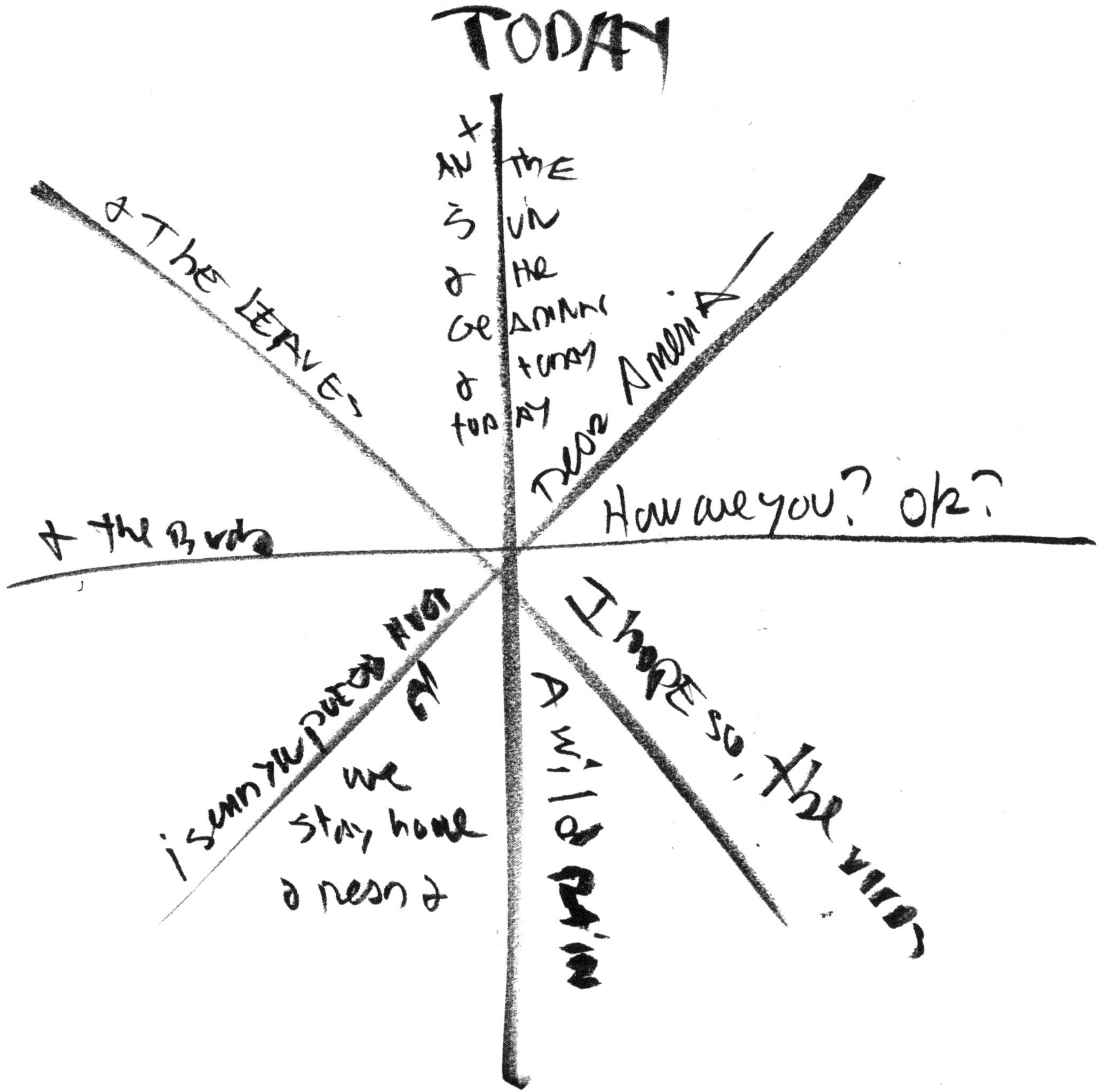
TODAY
& THE LEAVES
How are you? OK?
I hope so, the
we
stay home

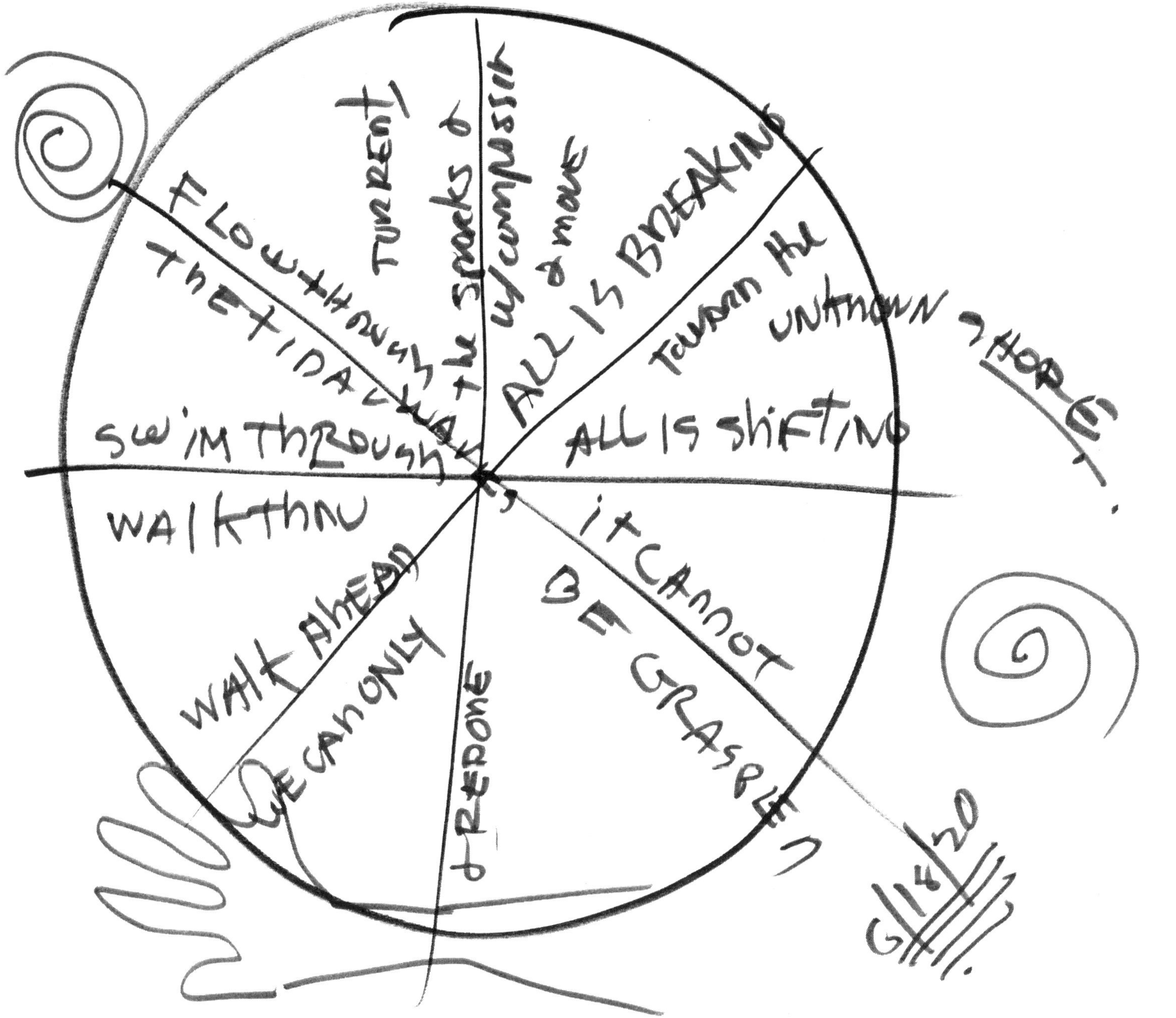

FLOW THROUGH
THE TIDAL WAVE
TURBULENT
the sparks of
w/ compassion
& move
ALL IS BREAKING
TOWARD THE
UNKNOWN HOPE
ALL IS SHIFTING
SWIM THROUGH
WALK THRU
WALK AHEAD
WE CAN ONLY
RESPOND
IT CANNOT
BE
GRASPED
6/18/20

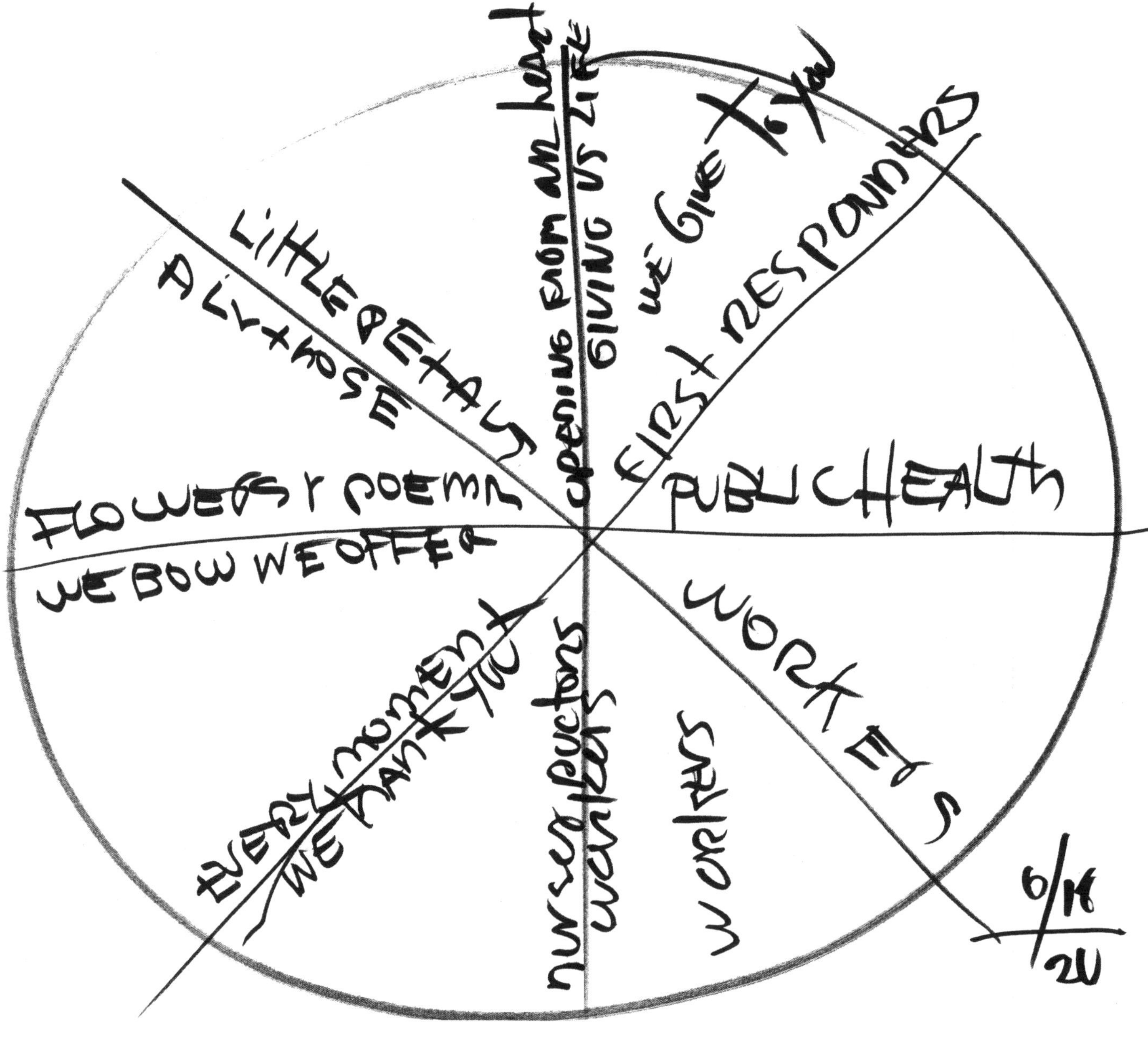

LITTLE PETALS
FLOWERS POEMS
WE BOW WE OFFER
OPENING FROM ALL heart
GIVING US LIFE
WE GIVE TO YOU
FIRST RESPONDERS
PUBLIC HEALTH
WORKERS
EVERY MOMENT
WE THANK YOU
nurses doctors
workers

SEE IT
DEMOCRACY
QUESTIONS POSSIBLE
ANSWERS YOUR ARE not GOING TO GET AN
HAVE it DO you
?
i AM HERE
& everywhere
where CARE
ANS WE R
FREEDOM where ARE
somehow YOU

WATCHING THE DIFFERENCE
THAT DOES NOT EXIST
GRASPING that which
CANNOT BE GRASPED
TELL ME
LIFE SHORT
WHAT IS THE
ULTIMATE
REALITY??
COVID-19 STRIKES
GALAXIES END
MISINFORMATION
THE WRONG WAY
FLOODS
CHANGING IN
CLIME CHANGE
OUT OF CONTROL
WARS & GUN &
ANIMALS WITHER
THE PATH
7/29/20

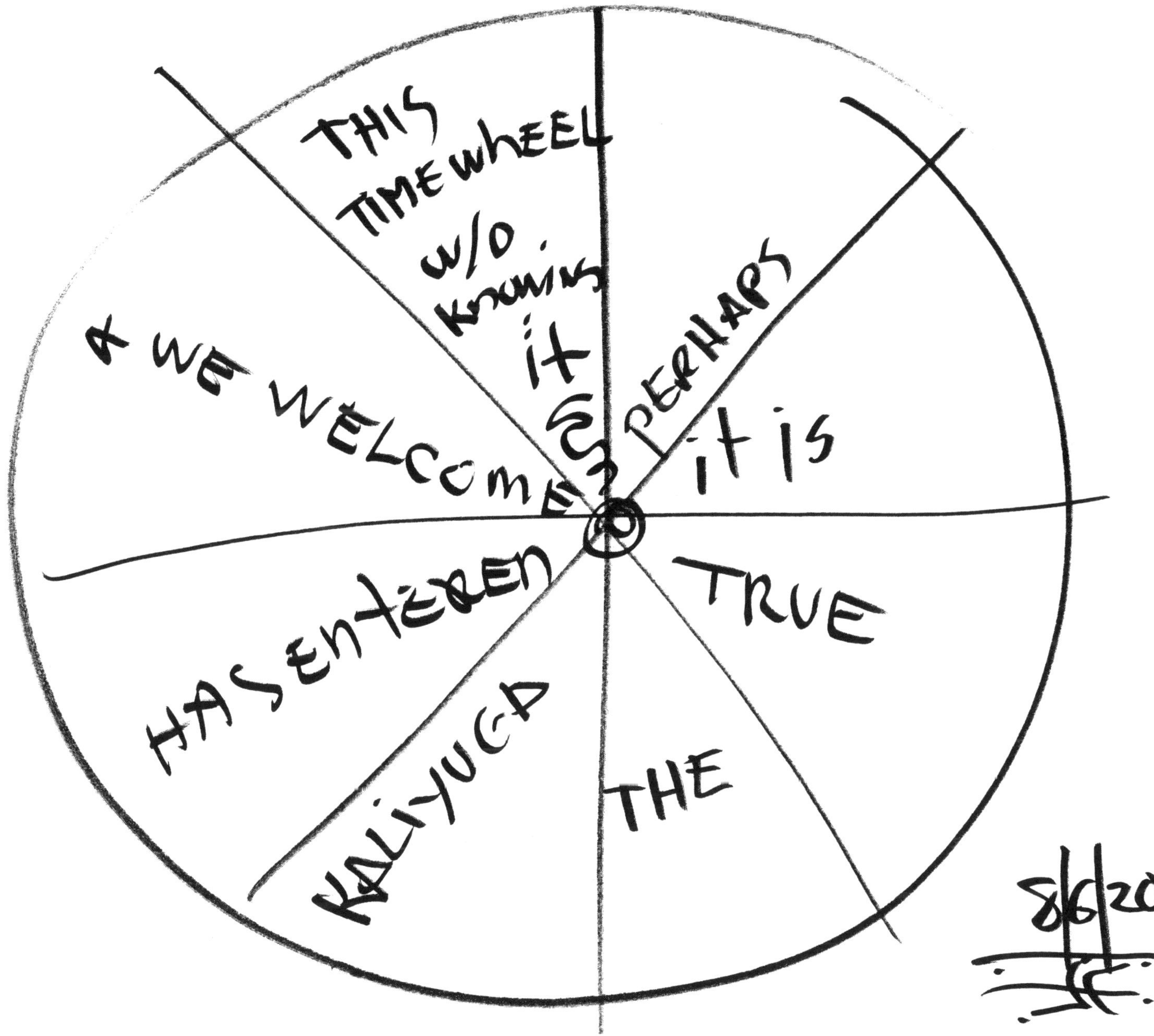
THIS
TIMEWHEEL
w/o
knowing
it
&
PERHAPS
it is
TRUE
THE
KALIYUGA
HAS entered
& WE WELCOME
8/6/20

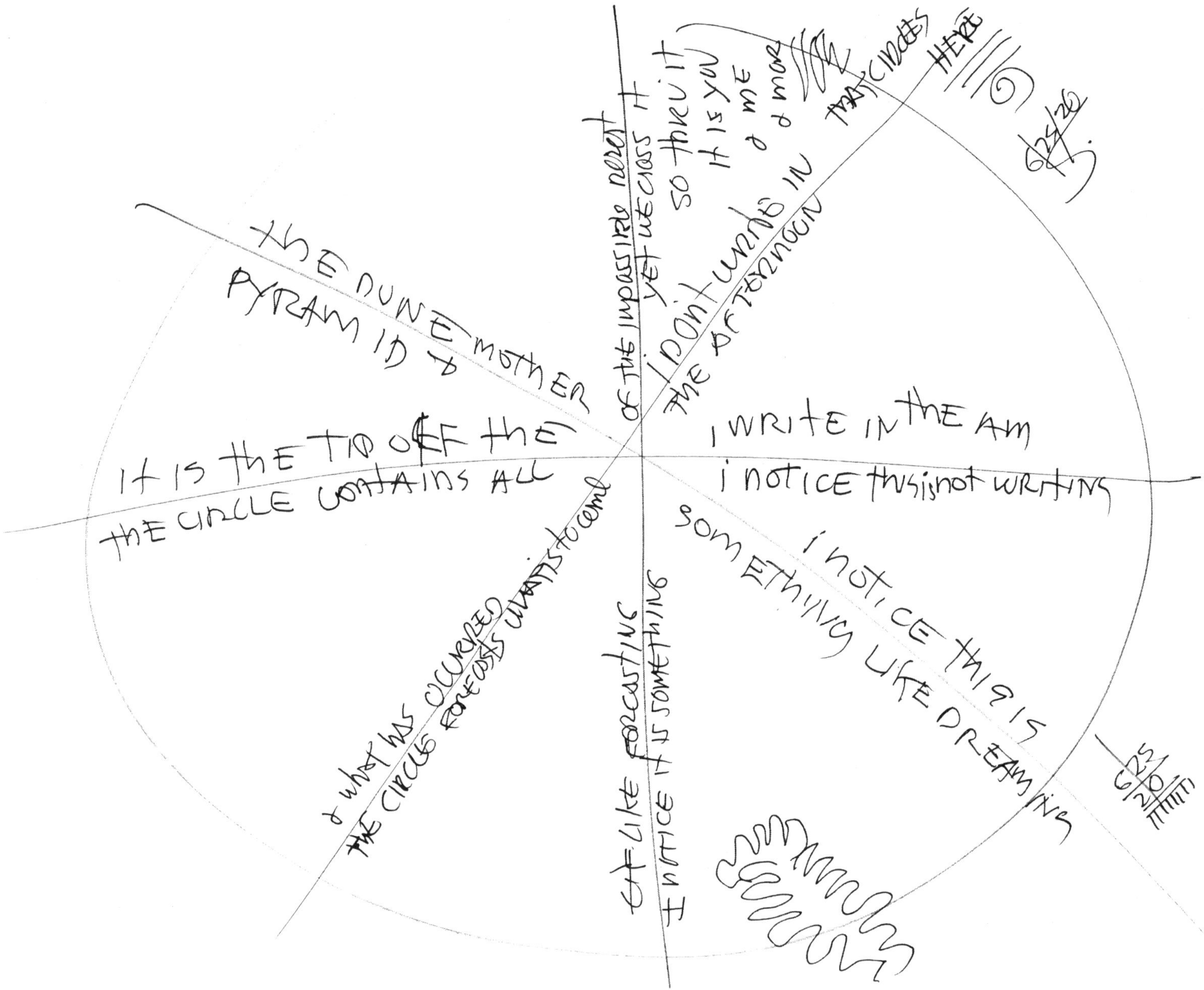
the dune mother
pyramid &
of the impossible desert
yet we cross it
so thru it
it is you
& me
& more
i don't write in
the afternoon
transcendes
HERE
6/25/20
i write in the am
i notice this is not writing
i notice this is
something like dreaming
6/25/20
it like forecasting
i notice it is something
& what has occurred
the circle forecasts what is to come
it is the tip of the
the circle contains all

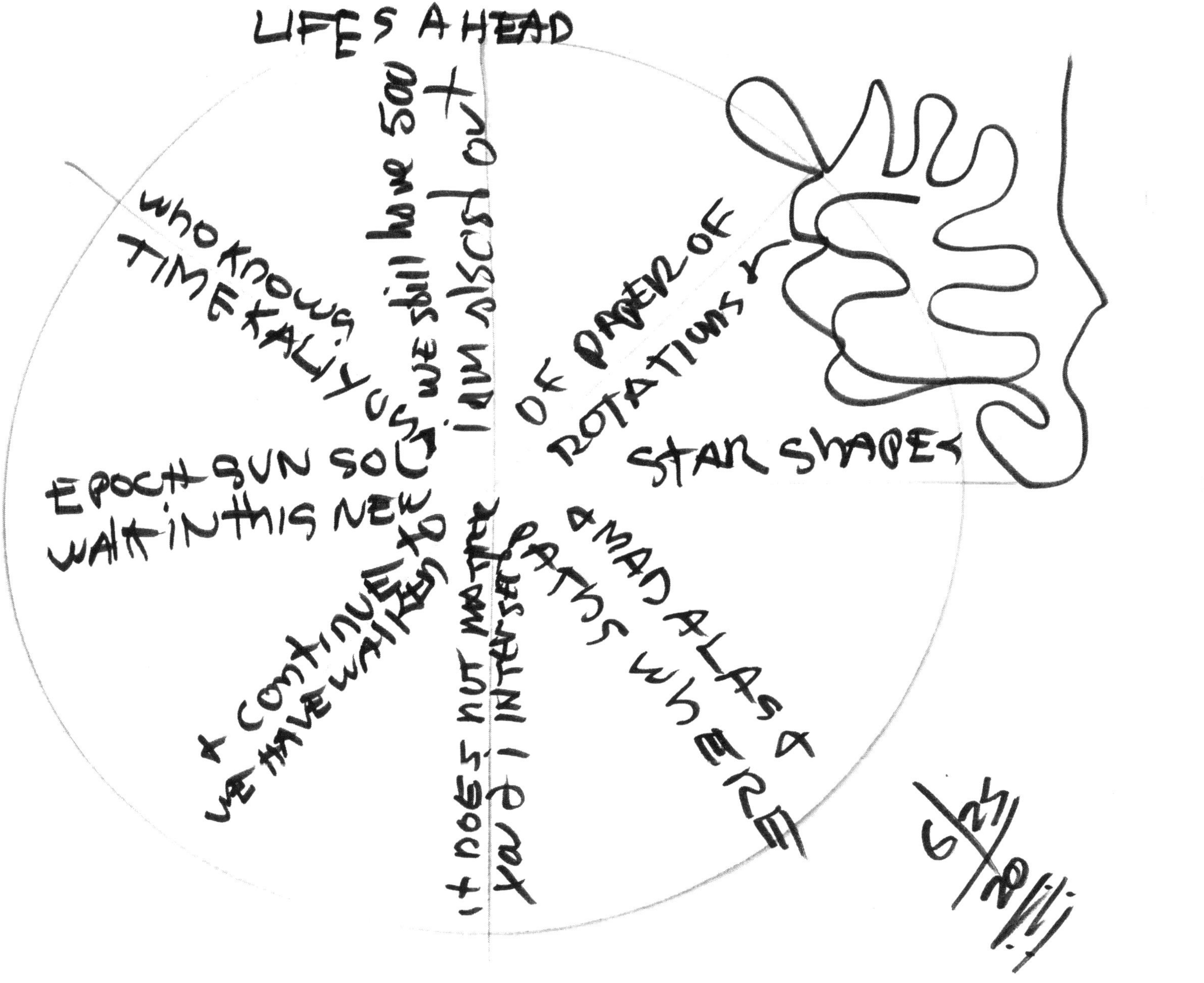

LIFES A HEAD
who knows
TIME KALIYUGS
we still have 500
OF PAPER OF
ROTATIONS
STAR SHAPES
EPOCH SUN SOL
WALK IN THIS NEW
& CONTINUE
WE HAVE WALKED TO
IT DOES NOT MATTER
PATHS WHERE
& MANDALAS &
6/25/2011

iAUNWibiNG on a wheel
w/ here
where
Here
customs
in is
a ball of
water that
the news
speaks

Oh
the
planet
oh
can
soar
oh car
beyon
Earth here
all of us
as one

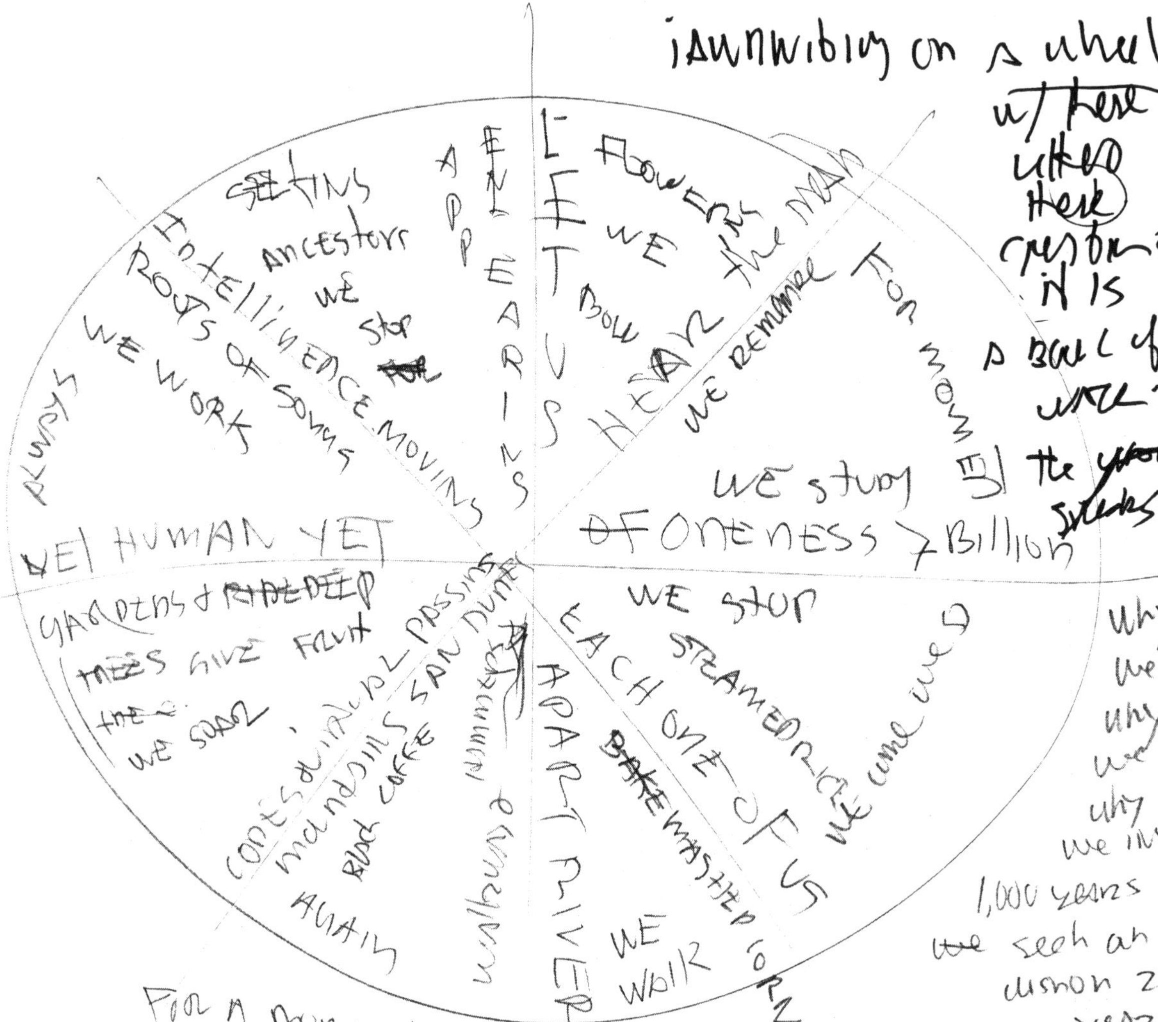

5/2/20

why?
we say
why
we whisper
why
we investigate
1,000 years
we seek an answer
wisdom 2100
year we
transcend
then we
reach a first sob

FOR A MOMENT WE NOTICE THE SUFFERING
WHAT DO WE SAY WHAT DO WE DO

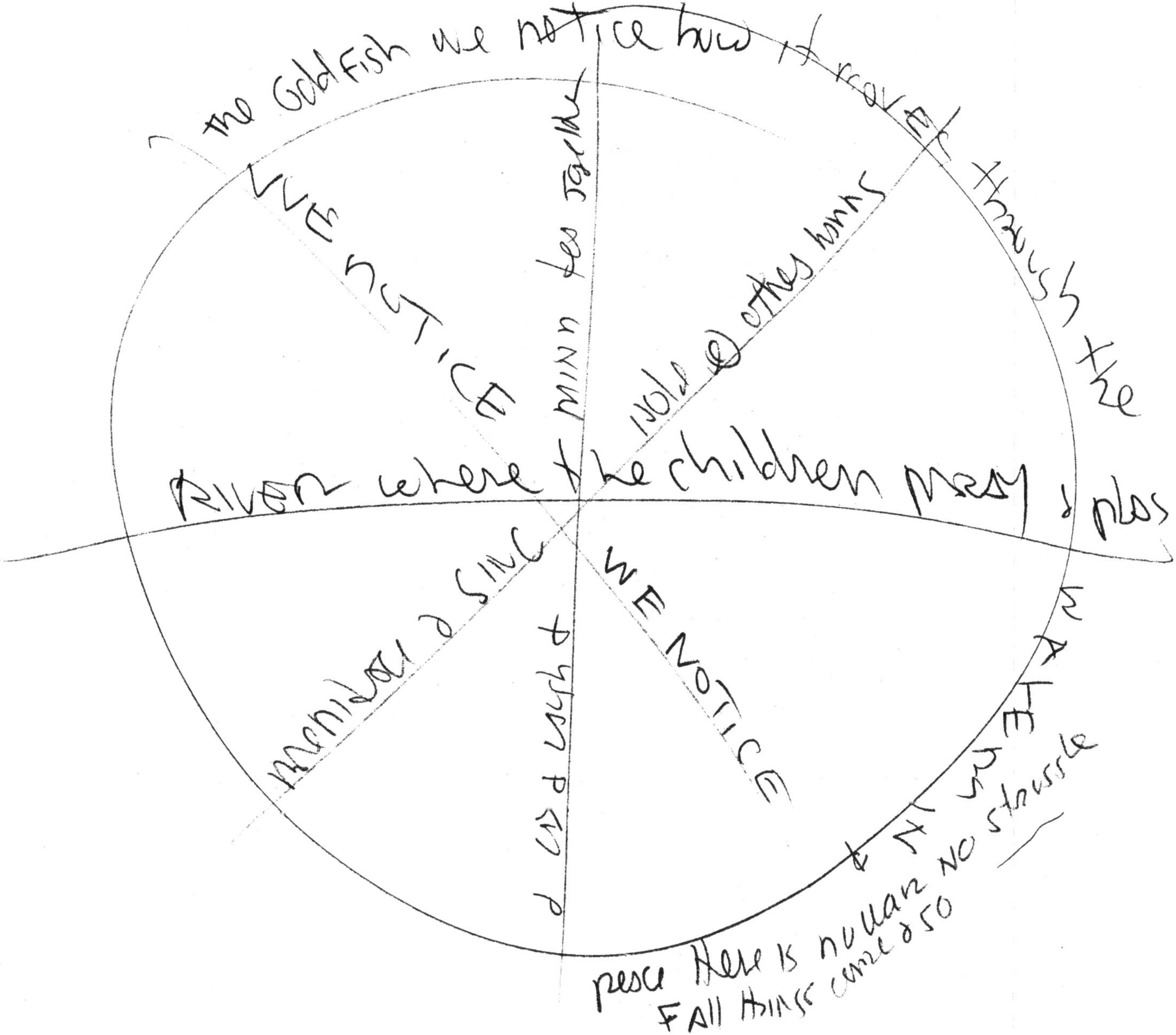
the Goldfish we notice how it moves through the
river where the children pray & play
WE NOTICE
hold @ others hands
WE NOTICE
WATER
& laugh & cry
peace there is no war no struggle
& all things come & go

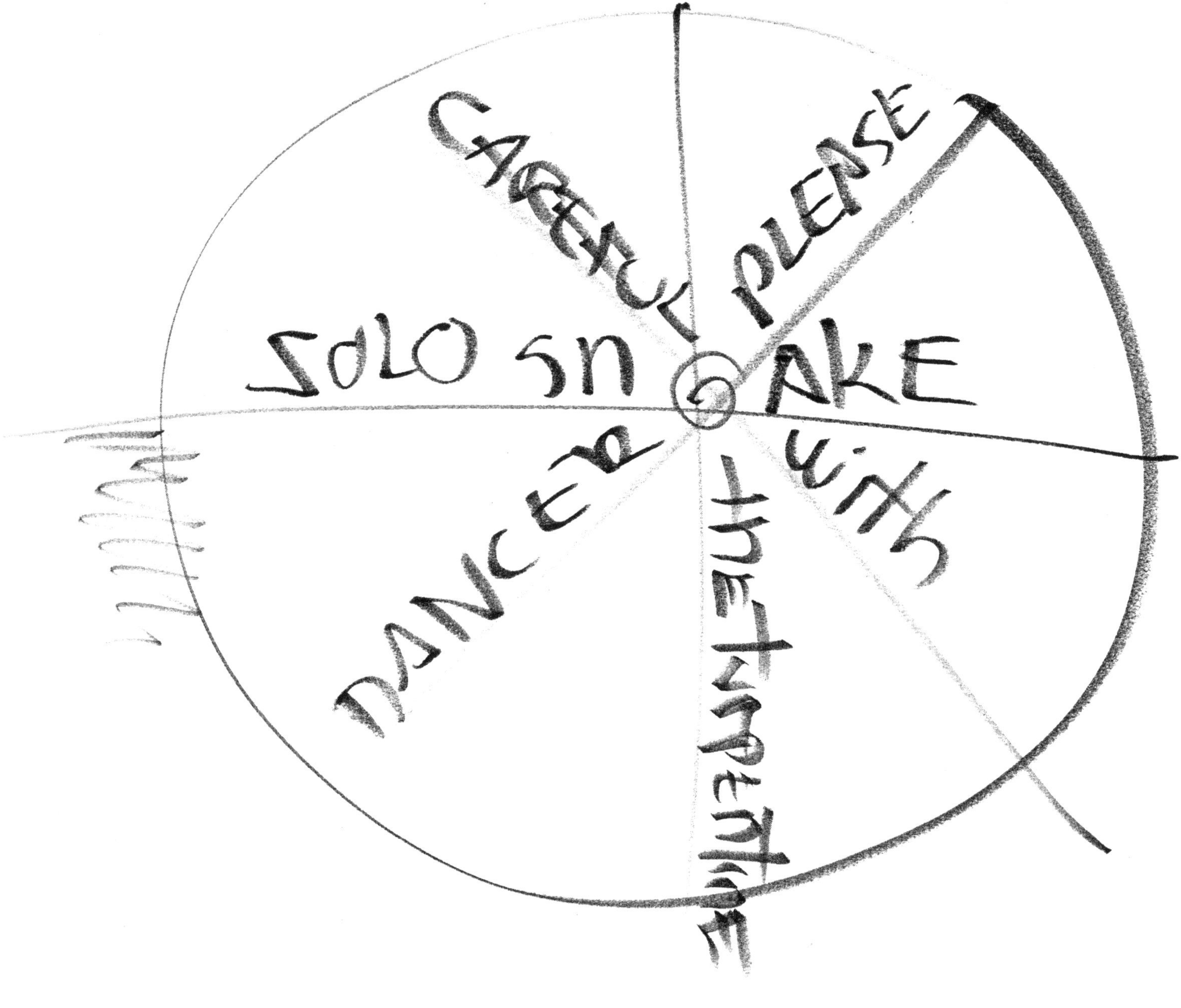
CAREFUL
PLEASE
SOLO SN
AKE
with
the turpentine
DANCER

WE MOVE WE
CHURN WE TURN
OUR TORSO WE LIFT
OUR LEGS & TURN OUR FEET
WE SCRAPE OUR ANKLE &
PRESS OUR THIGHS & OUR BREAST
TOUCHES & OUR ARMS & FEET
PUSH THE FORCES WE SHAPE
COUNTER FORCES SHAPING
AGAIN A CITY A SELF A
COLLECTIVE LIVES & LIVES
OF PEACE NON.VIOLENCE
& LOVE UNITY

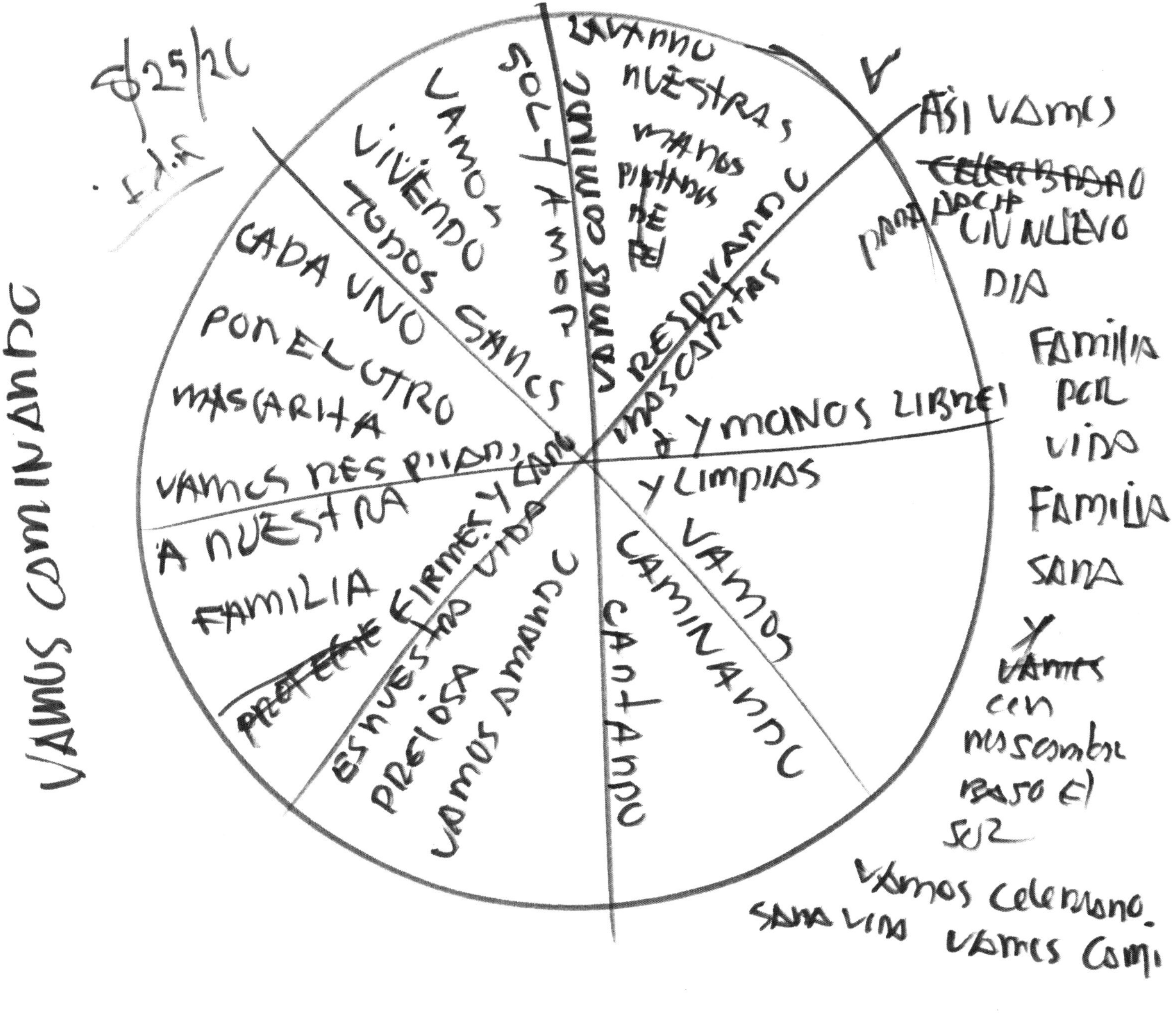

VAMOS CAMINANDO
25/20
LAVAMOS NUESTRAS MANOS PINTADAS DE FE
VAMOS CAMINANDO
SOL Y AMOR
VAMOS VIVIENDO TODOS SANOS
CADA UNO POR EL OTRO MASCARITA
VAMOS RESPIRANDO
A NUESTRA FAMILIA
FIRMES Y
ES NUESTRA VIDA PRECIOSA
VAMOS AMANDO
CANTANDO
CAMINANDO
VAMOS
Y LIMPIAS
Y MANOS LIBRES
RESPIRANDO MASCARITAS
ASÍ VAMOS
UN NUEVO DIA
FAMILIA POR VIDA
FAMILIA SANA
Y
VAMOS CELEBRANDO
SANA VIDA
VAMOS CAMI

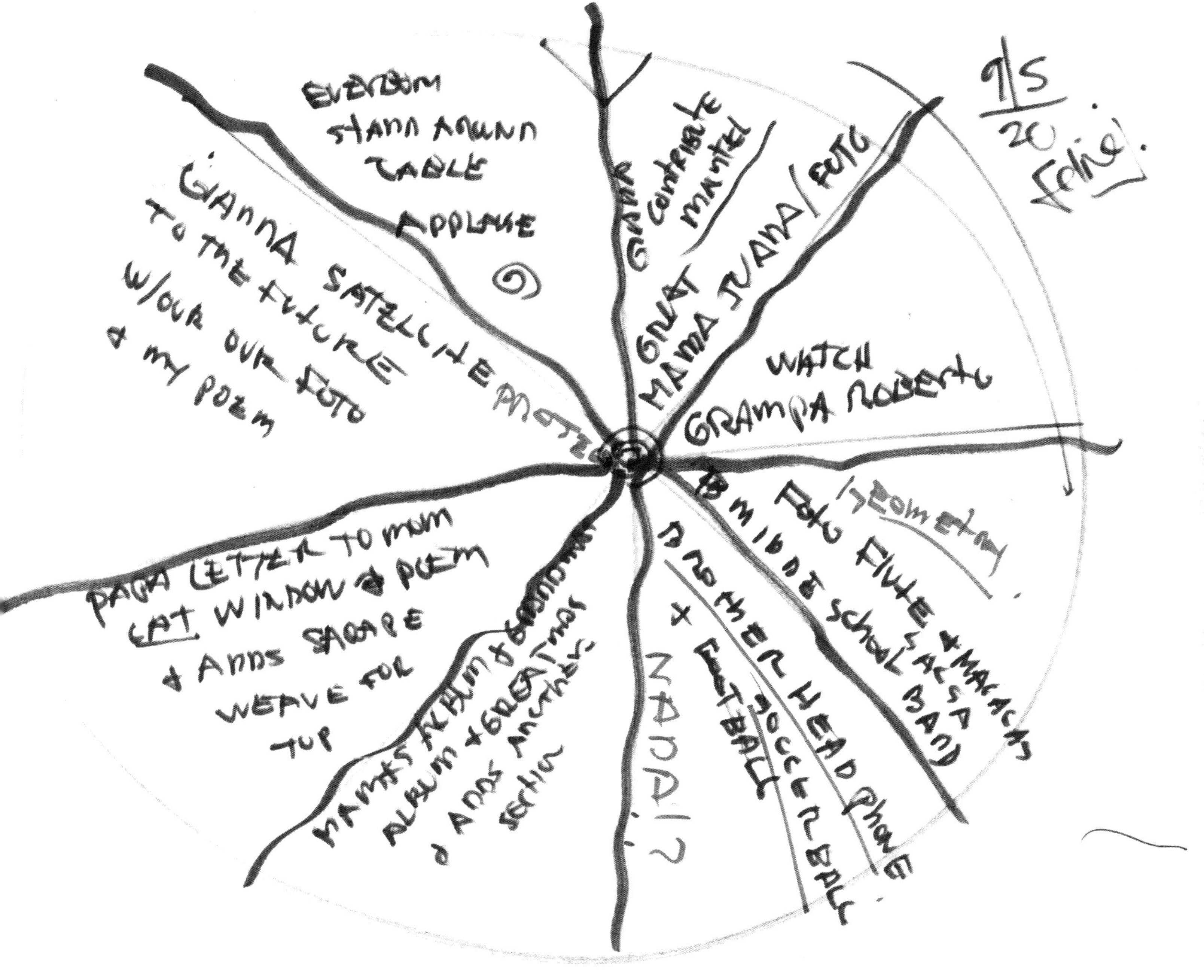

9/5/20 Feliz
STAND AROUND TABLE
APPLAUSE
GIANNA SATELLITE
TO THE FUTURE
W/OUR OUR FOTO
& MY POEM
CONTRIBUTE MANTEL
GREAT MAMA JUANA/FOTO
WATCH GRAMPA ROBERTO
GEOMETRY
FOTO FLUTE + MARACAS
MIDDLE SCHOOL SALSA BAND
BROTHER HEAD PHONE
+ SOCCER BALL
NADA?
PAPA LETTER TO MOM
CAT WINDOW & POEM
& ADDS SARAPE
WEAVE FOR TOP
& ADDS ANOTHER SECTION

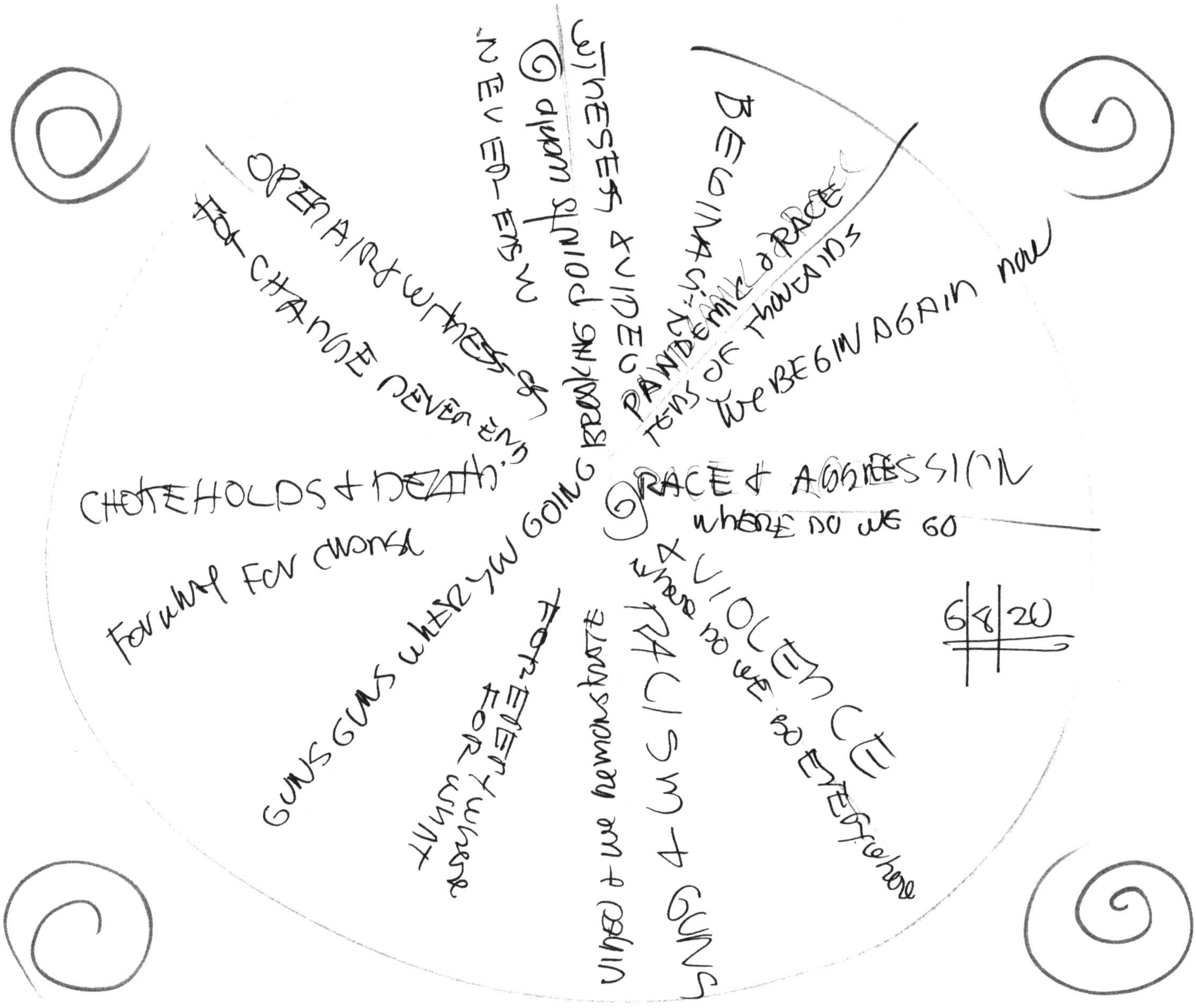

OPEN AIR WITNESS
FOR CHANGE NEVER ENDS
CHOKEHOLDS & DEATH
FOR WHAT FOR CHANGE
NEVER ENDS
BREAKING POINT
BEGINNING
PANDEMIC & RACE
TENS OF THOUSANDS
WE BEGIN AGAIN NOW
RACE & AGGRESSION
WHERE DO WE GO
& VIOLENCE
where do we go everywhere
RACISM & GUNS
VIDEO & we demonstrate
FOR EVERYWHERE FOR WHAT
GUNS GUNS WHERE YOU GOING
6 8 20

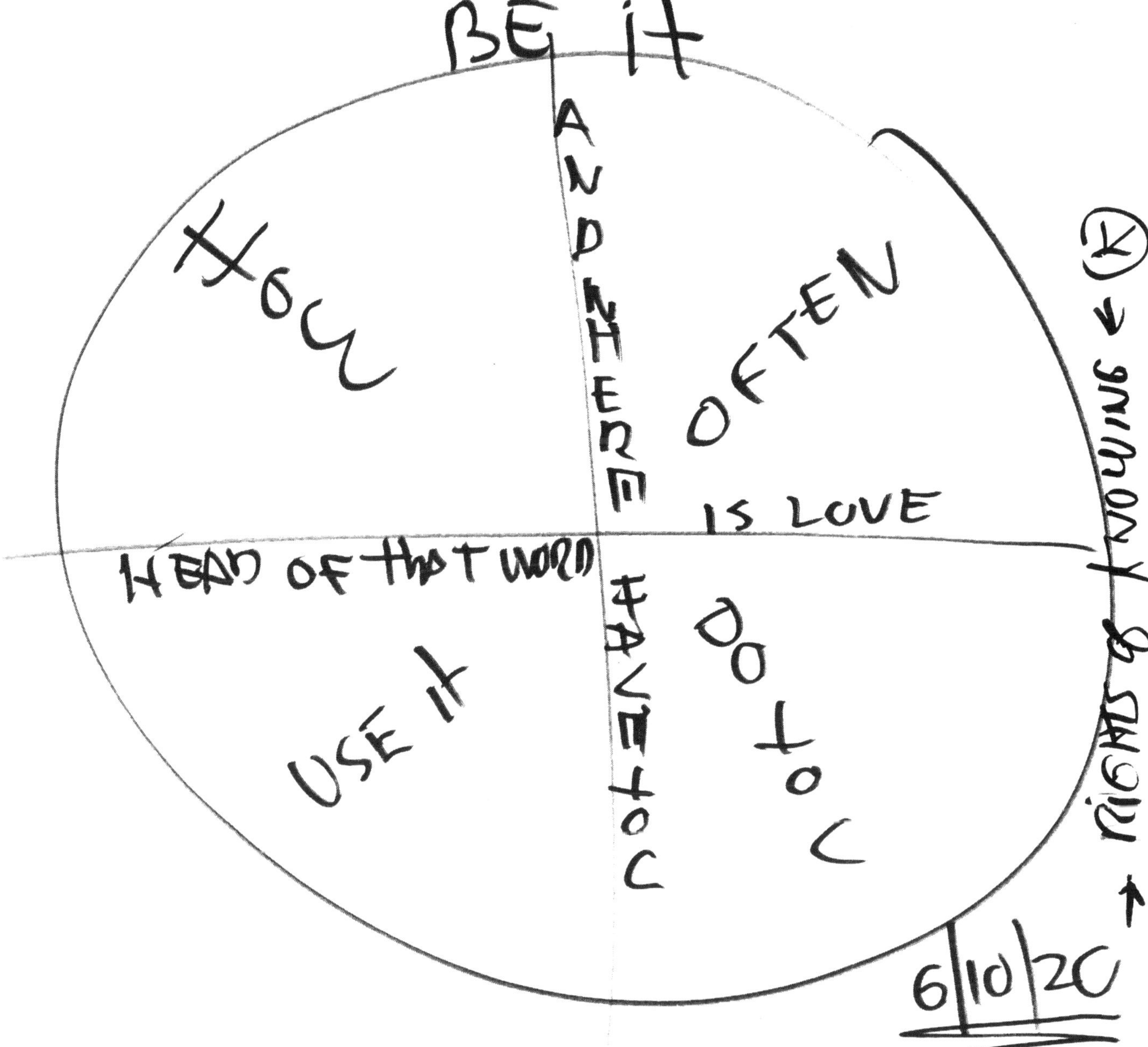

BE it
HOW
AND WHERE
OFTEN
IS LOVE
HEAD OF THAT WORD
USE IT
HAVE TO C
DO TO C
RIGHTS & KNOWING
K
6 10 20

MEDITATION II
BECOME THE OTHER

It cannot be grasped
Lu Chi the ancient one said
you must task emptiness
the webbed wheel of the cosmos
move move move w/one
touch/finger/breath
breathe now
spin
spin spin

into this
new moment
into this
new life
of all life
all around everywhere life and things
kindness
mercy let us pour

one voice
all of our voices
all of our lives

all silence
all change
all stars becoming
one star
thru flames and night and blue
solar winds

we are made of freedom
yes

the sky oceans
& every living being
stand up and sing

kindness
kindness
kindness

so many lives
the wheel turns
you turn
the infinite blank trembles
we begin again
we touch 500 lives
become
become
become
the
other

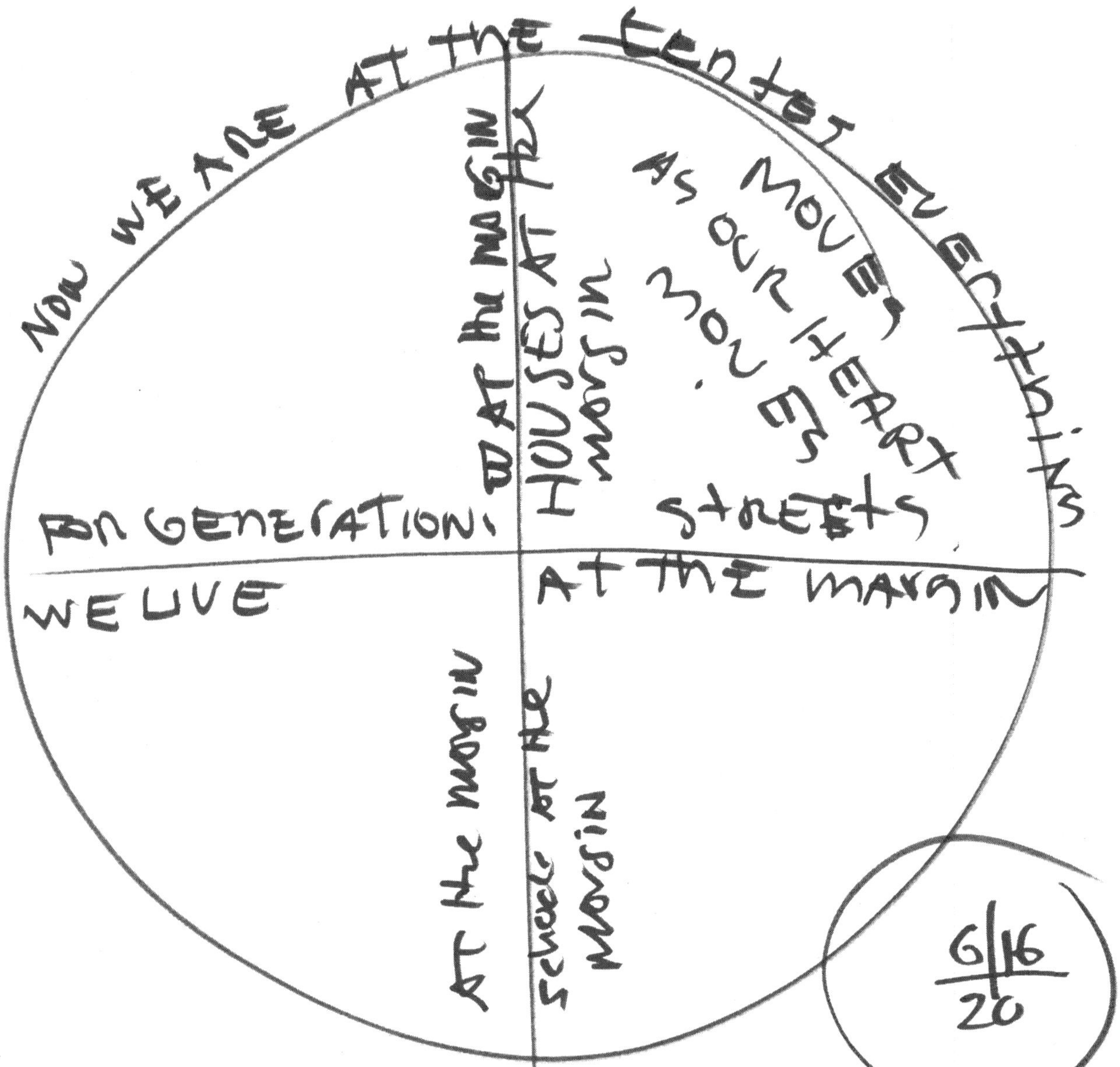
NOW WE ARE AT THE CENTER
EVERYTHING MOVES,
AS OUR HEART MOVES
STREETS
AT THE MARGIN
HOUSES AT THE MARGIN
AT THE MARGIN
FOR GENERATIONS
WE LIVE
AT THE MARGIN
AT THE MARGIN
SCHOOLS AT THE MARGIN
6/16/20

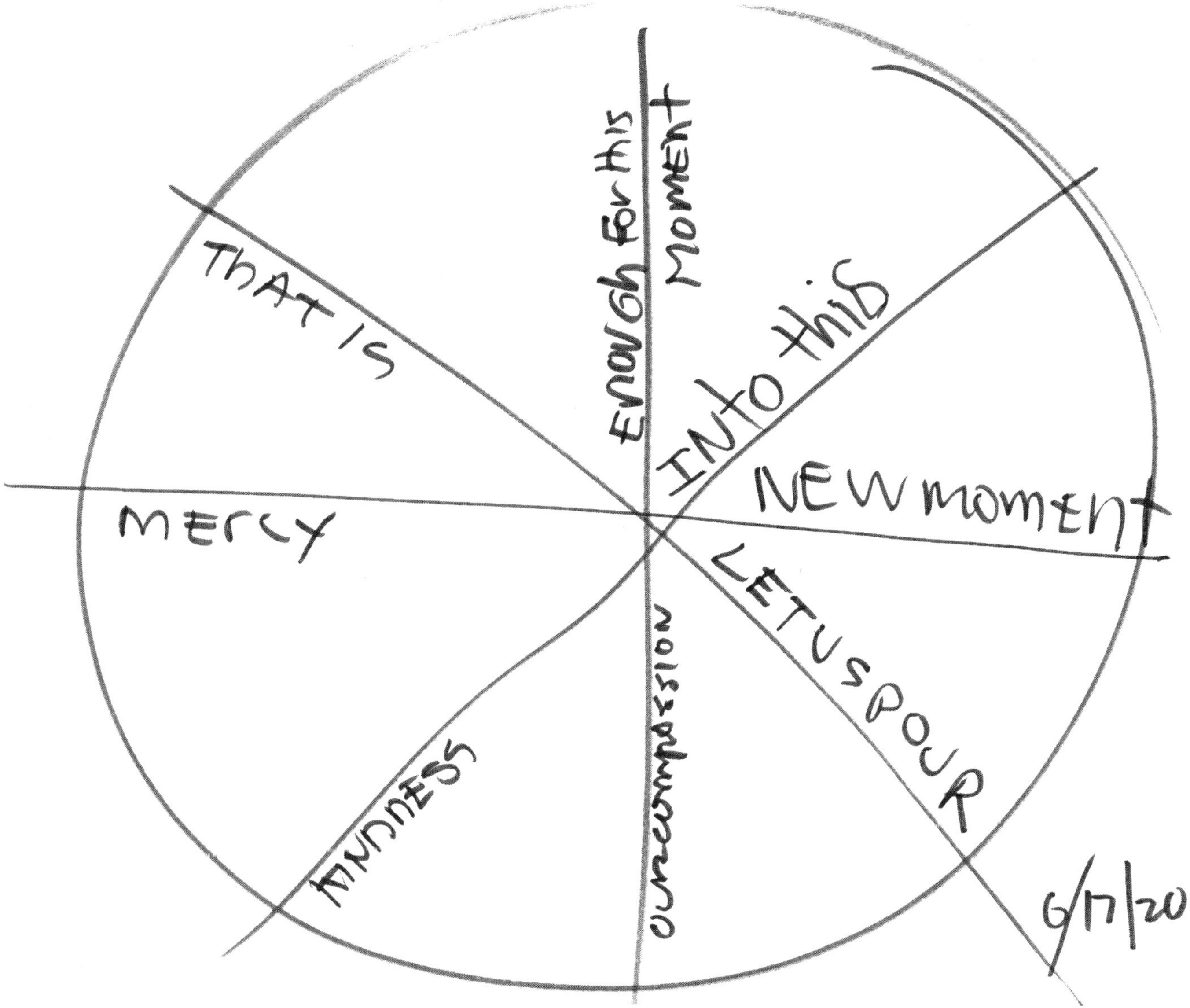
INTO THIS
NEW MOMENT
LET US POUR
our compassion
KINDNESS
MERCY
THAT IS
ENOUGH for this
MOMENT
6/17/20

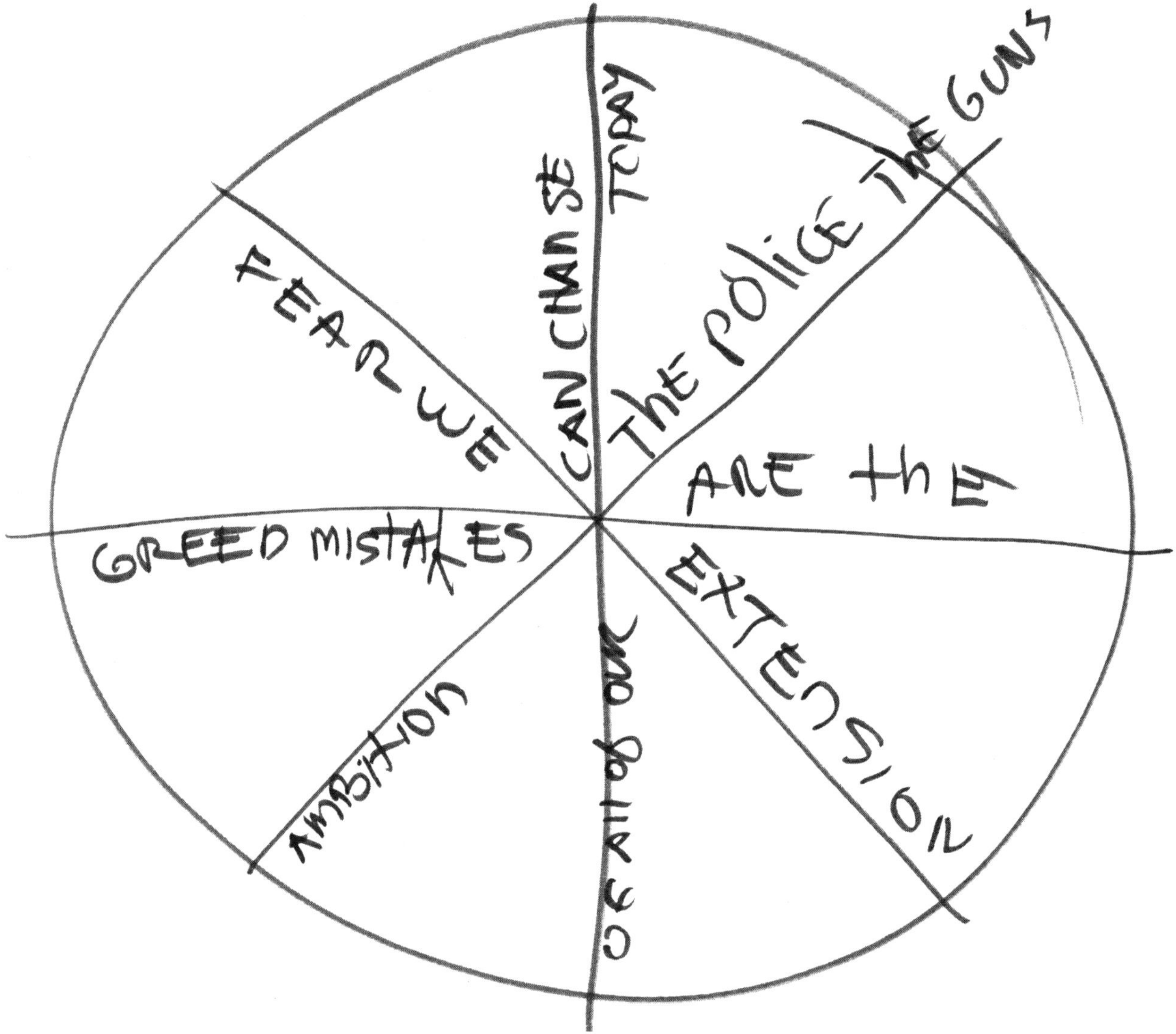
THE POLICE THE GUNS
ARE THE
EXTENSION
OF ALL OF OUR
AMBITION
GREED MISTAKES
FEAR WE
CAN CHANGE
TODAY

IN A TIME

OF ~~TH~~ ~~our~~ ABANDONMENT
ABADMENT

BY THE GOVERNING EXTERNAL

POWERS THAT BE
WE MUST FORTIFY &
NOURISH OUR

INTENSE CREATIVITY
INTENSE COMPASSION
INTENSE RESHAPING

OF OUR ENERGY

6/17/20

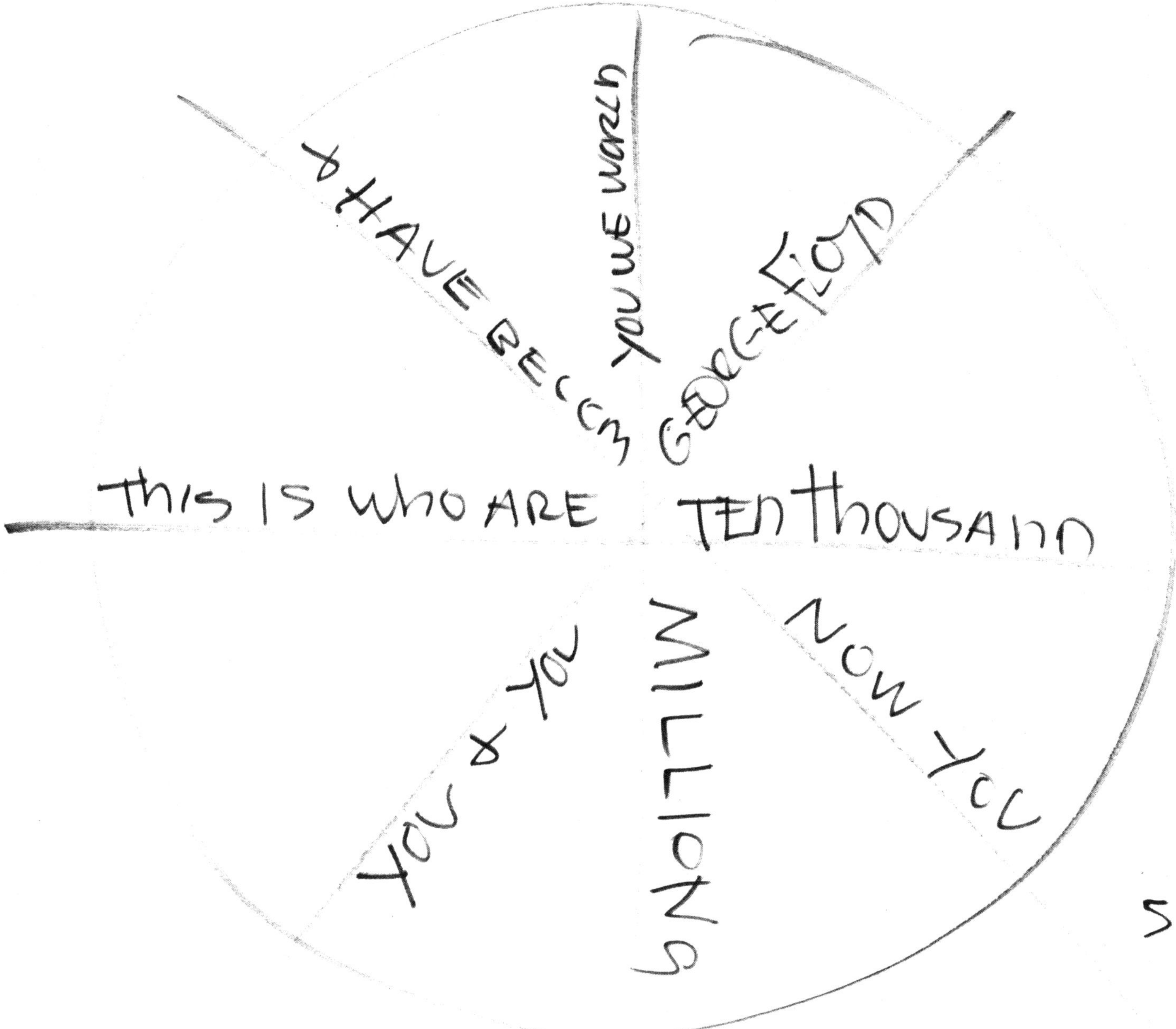
This is who are
& have becom
you we world
George Floyd
Ten thousand
Now you
Millions
You & you

5/13/20

ARE FALLING
BECOMING
PETALS
BOLD
SEEING SEEING
BLOSSOMS
PEACE
A new petal
EACH PETAL
The children
of THE mothers
TIME
NEW
BECOMING YOU
ALL THE
BECOMING
THE STREETS
THE WINDS
THE AIR
SHOWING
WORLD
REWALKING
THE
6/13/20

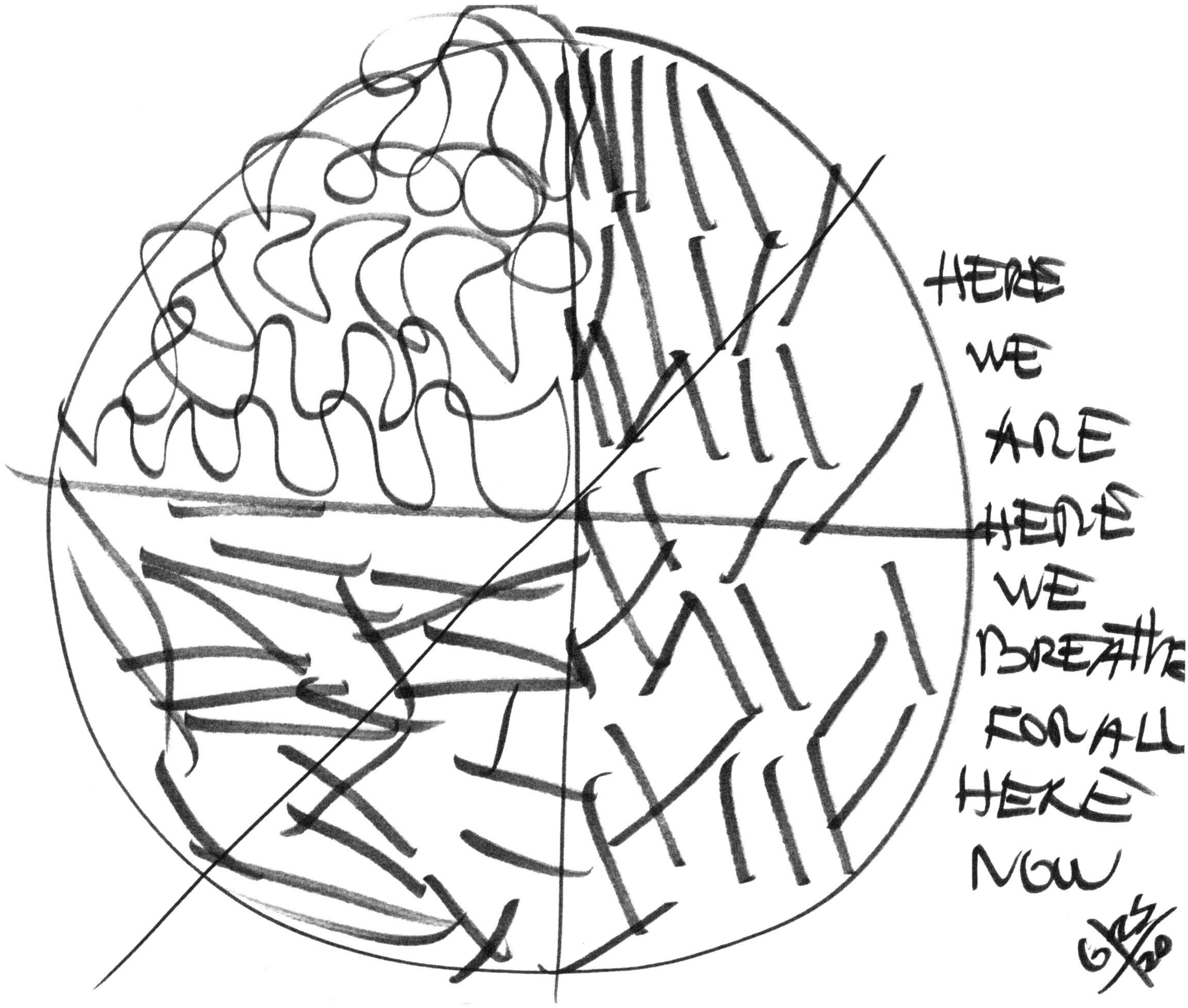
HERE
WE
ARE
HERE
WE
BREATHE
FOR ALL
HERE
NOW

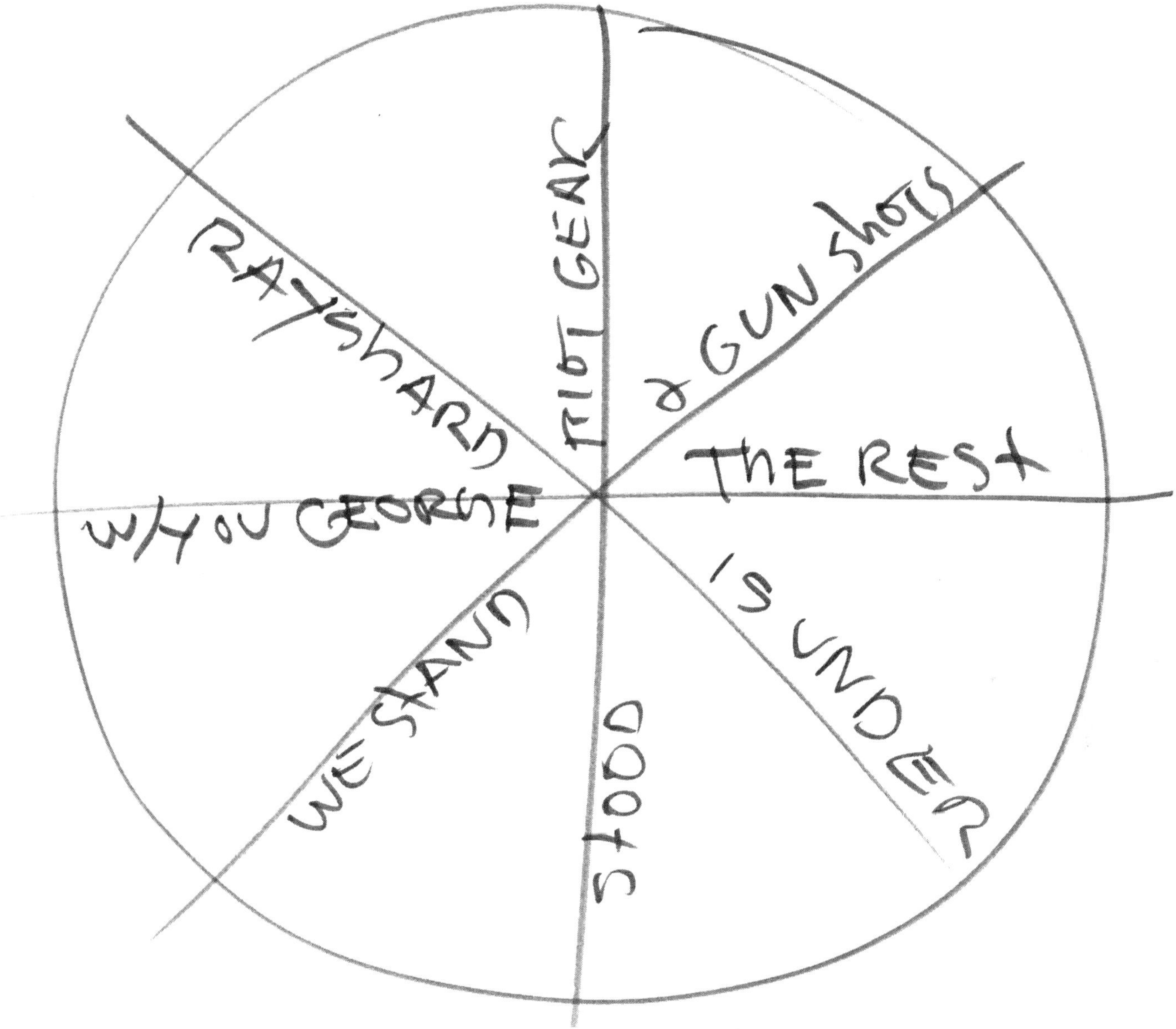
WE STAND
W/YOU GEORGE
RAYSHARD
RIOT GEAR
& GUN SHOTS
THE REST
IS UNDER
STOOD

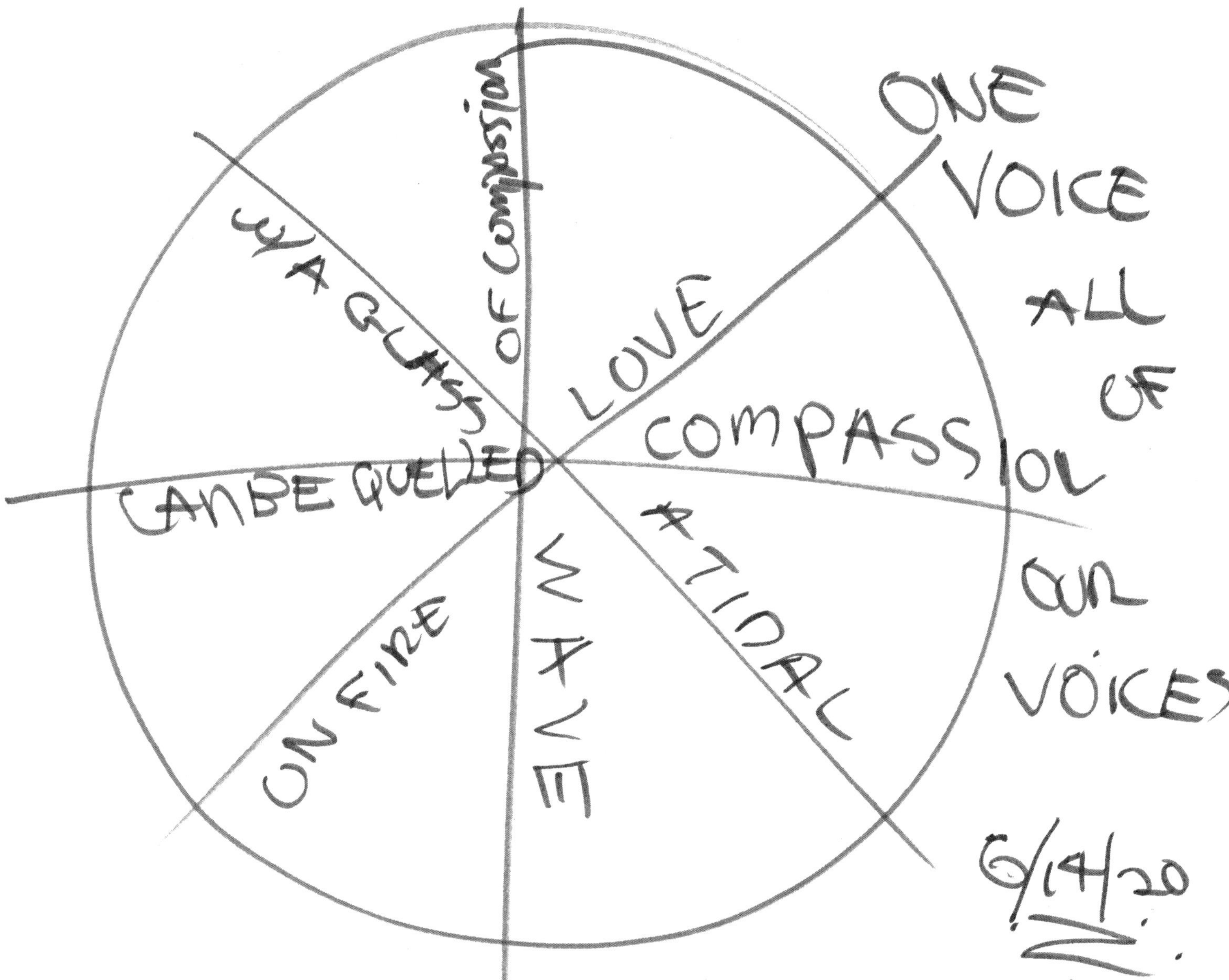
LOVE
COMPASSIOL
A TIDAL
WAVE
ON FIRE
CAN BE QUELLED
W/A GLASS
OF COMPASSION
ONE
VOICE
ALL
OF
OUR
VOICES
6/14/20

FREEDOM IS OUR NAME I WAS
ALWAYS OUR NAME
OUR HANDS ARE
MADE OF IT
OUR VOICES
ARE MADE
OF FREEDOM
OUR BODIES
ARE MADE OF
FREEDOM
FREEDOM
That is why when we
walk speak
listen dream
sit rise &
shout freedom
rains &
unites
all
suffering hearts

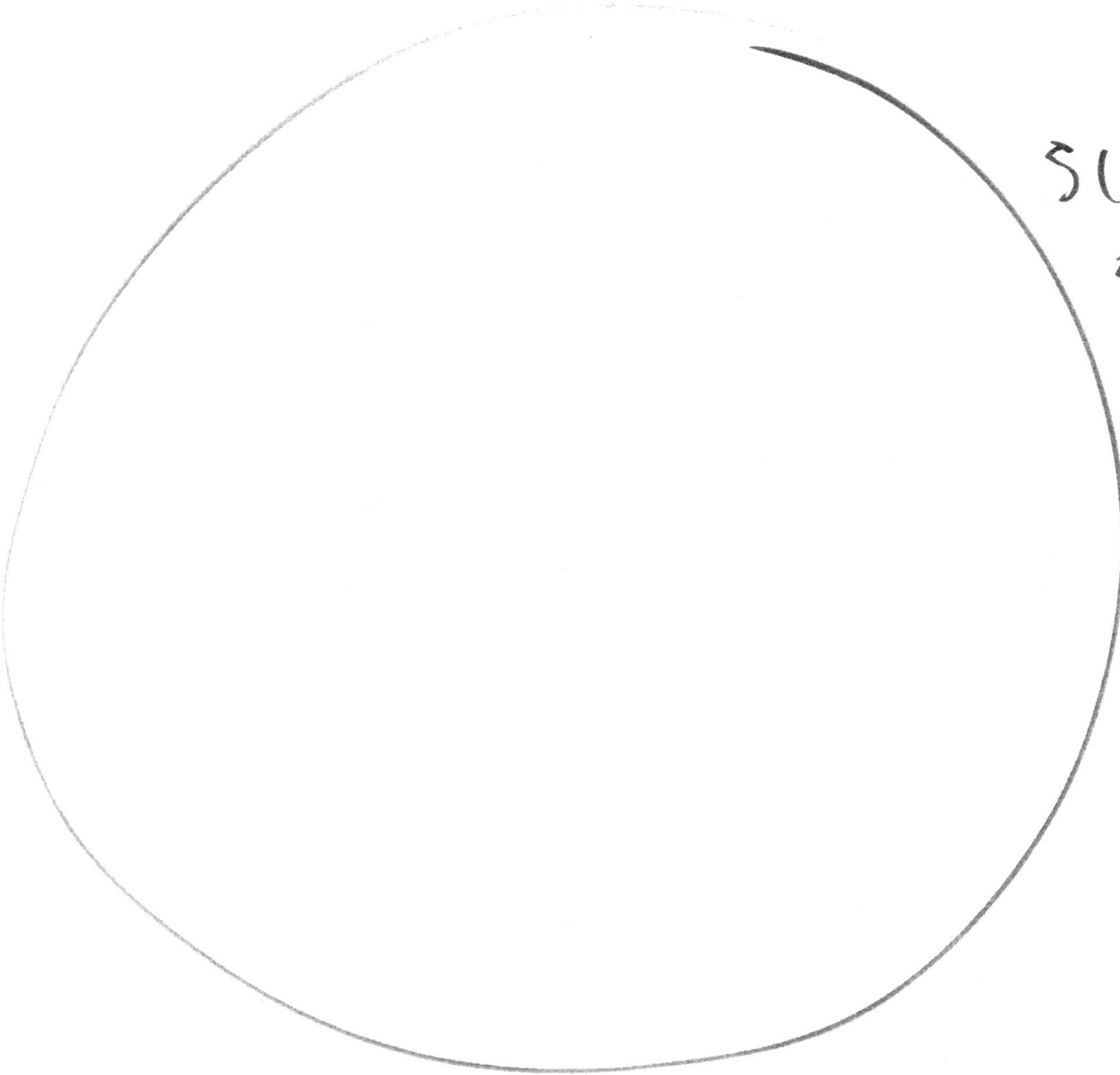

SUN
STUDIES
CLUB
HOUSE

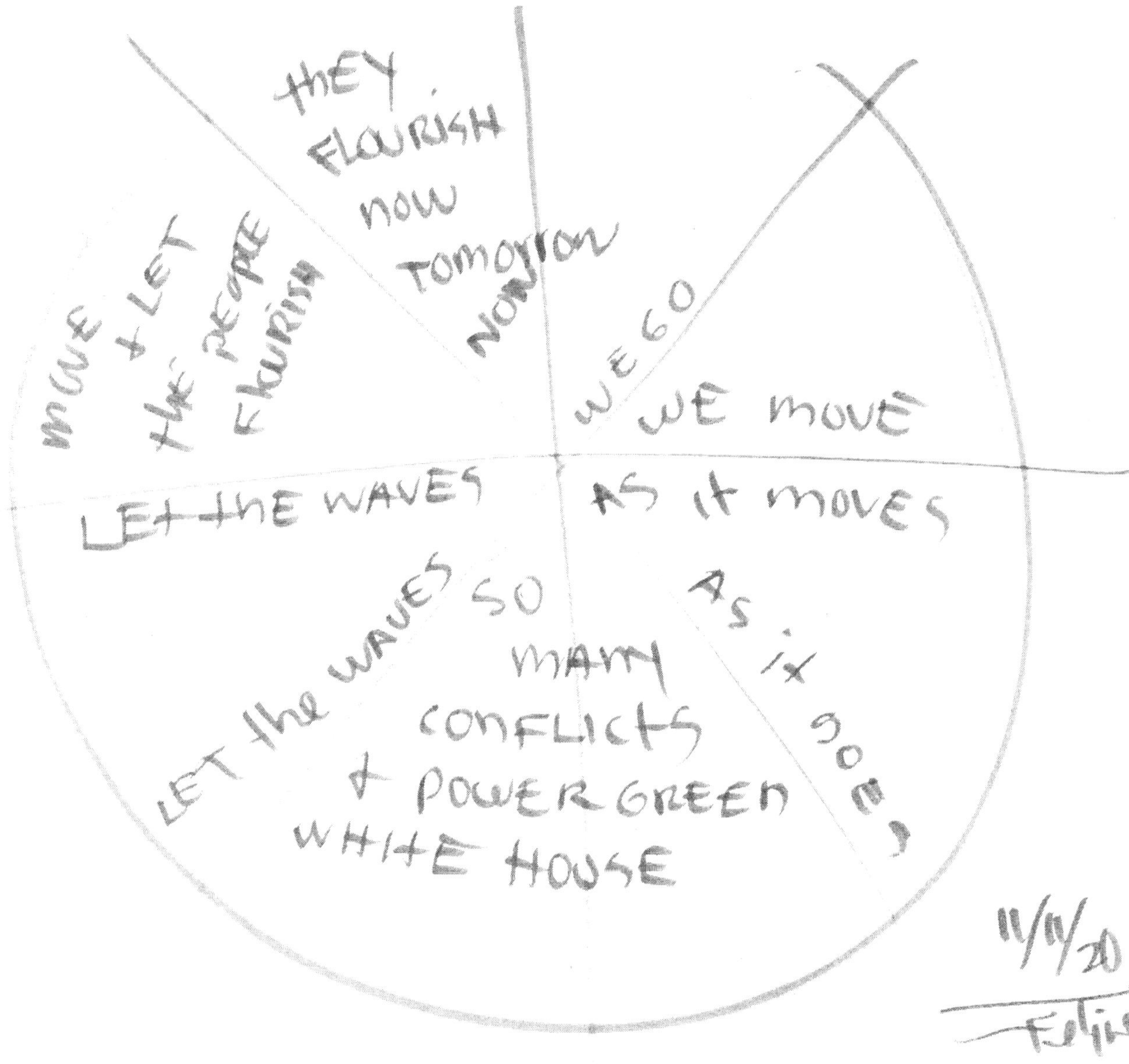
they FLOURISH now
TOMORROW NOW
MOVE & LET the PEOPLE FLOURISH
WE GO
WE MOVE
LET the WAVES
AS it MOVES
AS it GOES
LET the WAVES
SO many CONFLICTS & POWER GREED WHITE HOUSE
11/11/20

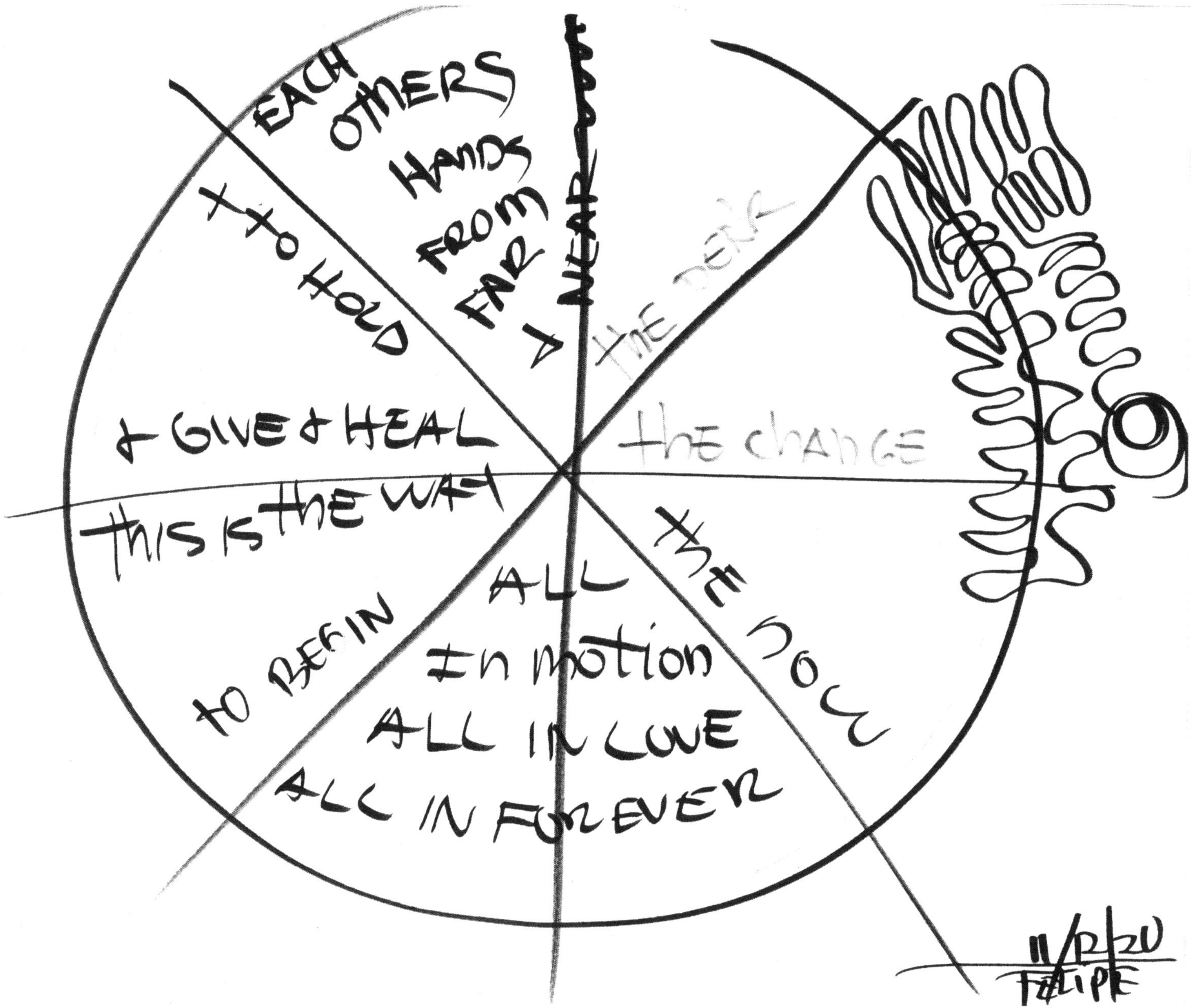
EACH OTHERS HANDS FROM FAR & NEAR
& TO HOLD
& GIVE & HEAL
THIS IS THE WAY
TO BEGIN
ALL IN MOTION
ALL IN LOVE
ALL IN FOREVER
THE NOW
THE DEAR
THE CHANGE
11/12/20
FELIPE

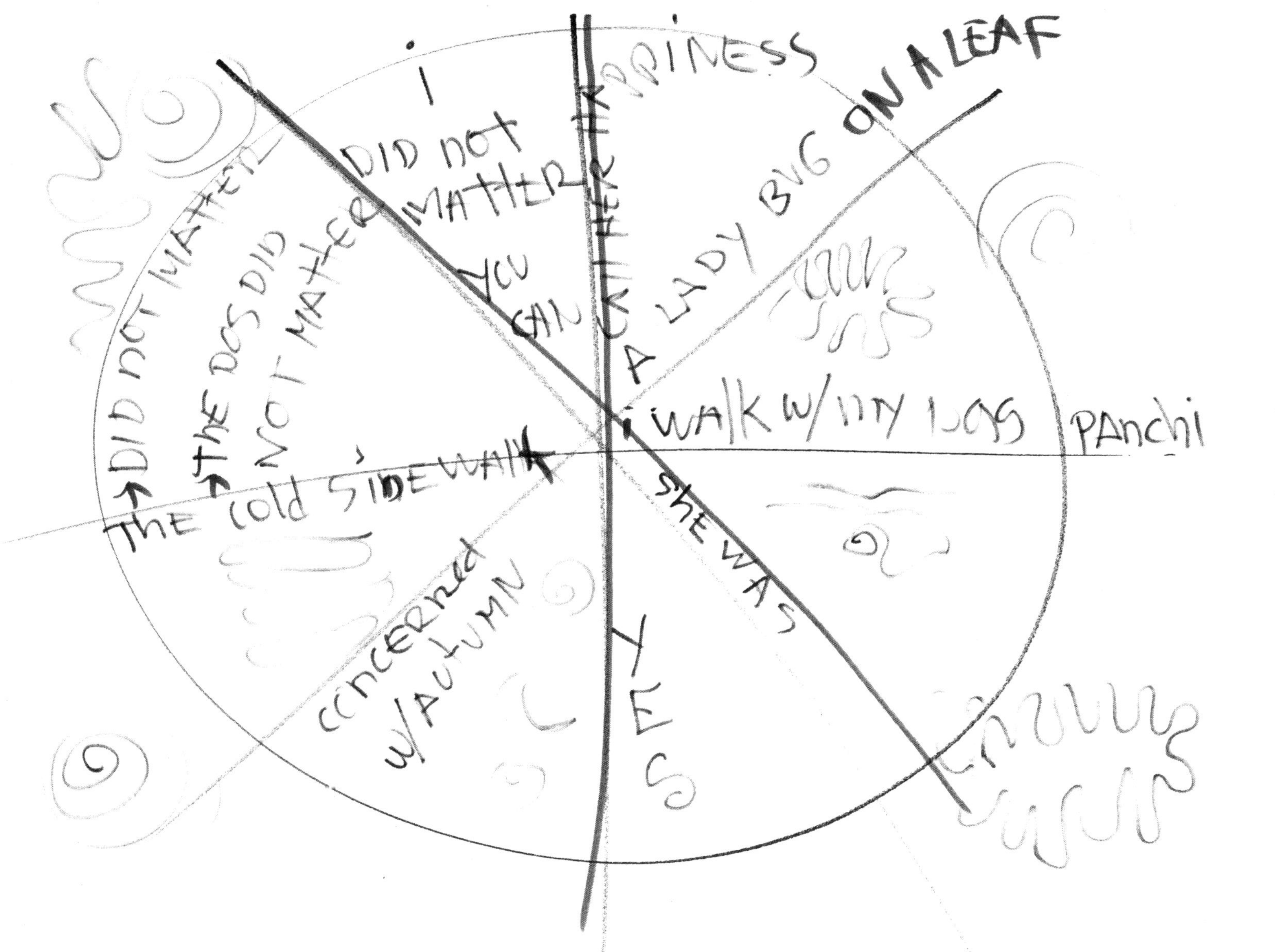
i
DID NOT
MATTER
HAPPINESS
ON A LEAF
A LADY BUG
YOU
CAN
i walk w/ my dog
Panchi
DID NOT MATTER
THE DOG DID
NOT MATTER
THE cold SIDEWALK
SHE WAS
concerned
w/ autumn
YES

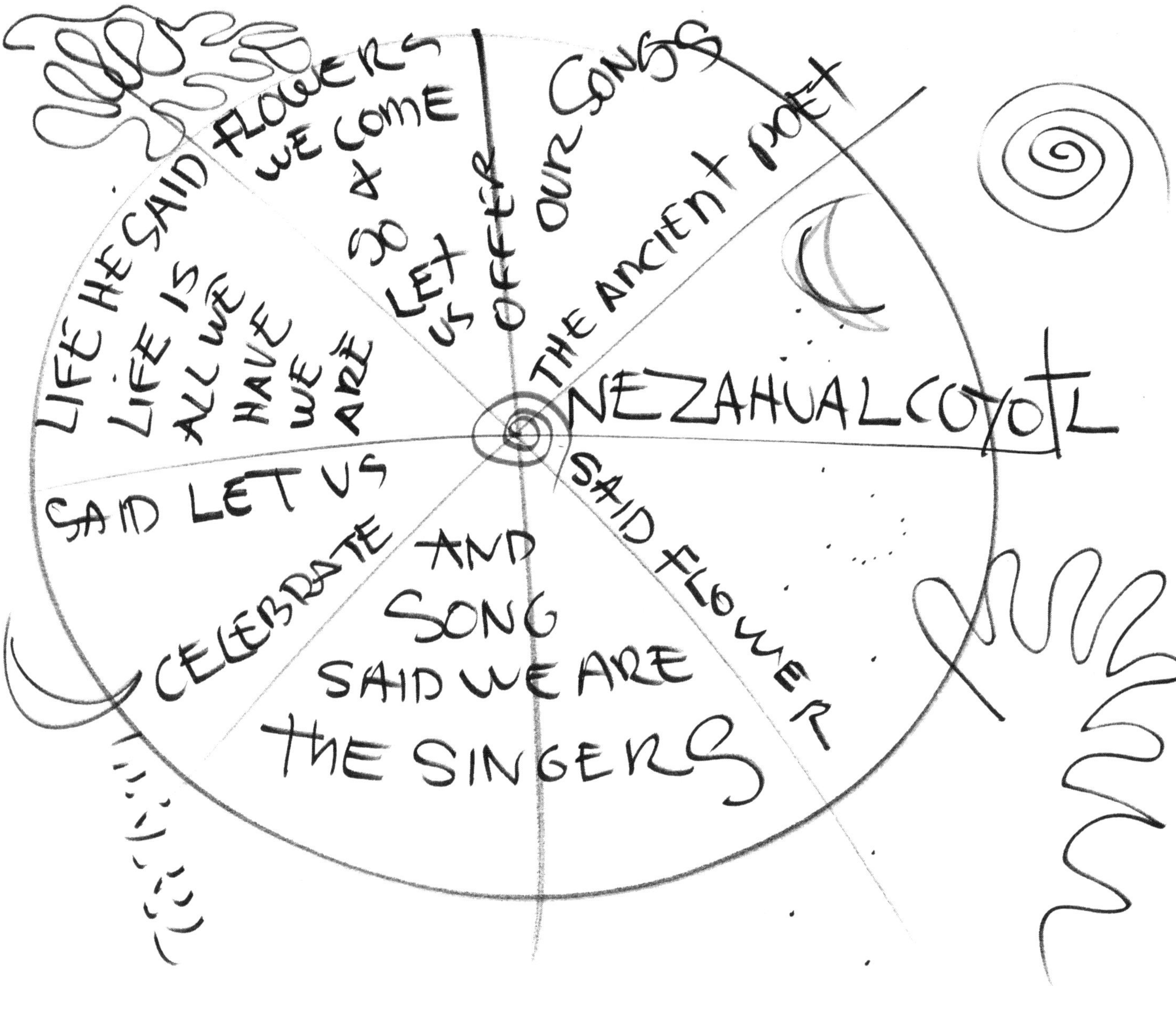
LIFE HE SAID FLOWERS
WE COME
&
SO LET US OFFER OUR SONGS
THE ANCIENT POET
NEZAHUALCOYOTL
SAID FLOWER
AND SONG
SAID WE ARE
THE SINGERS
LIFE IS ALL WE HAVE WE ARE
SAID LET US
CELEBRATE

ENGLISH VIBRATES

ACROSS MY TABLE

WHAT DO I DO ?

I FEEL LIKE AN

EMPANADA

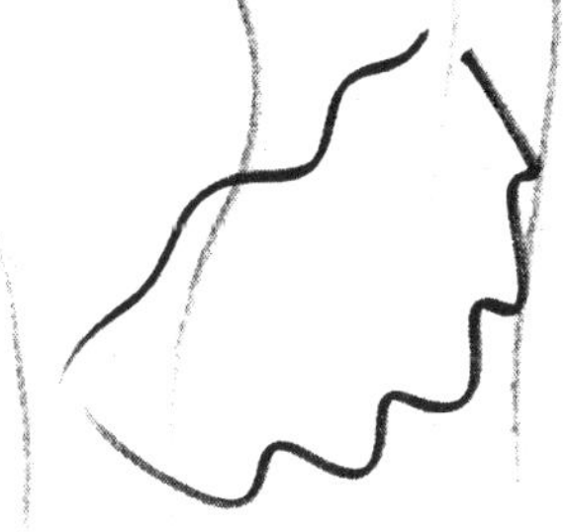

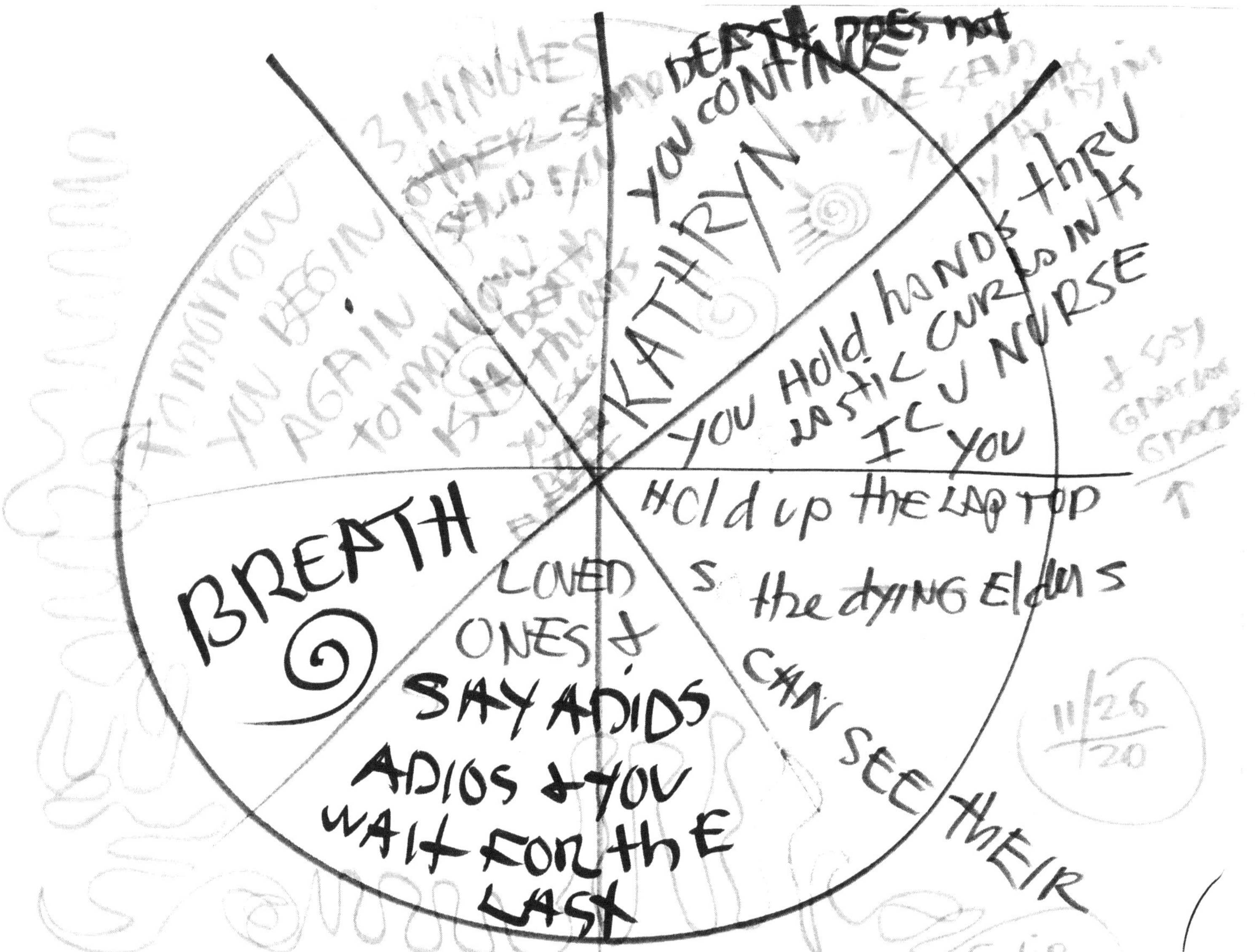

DEATH DOES NOT
YOU CONTINUE
KATHRYN
YOU Hold hands thru
ICU NURSE
YOU
Hold up the LAP TOP
the dying Elders
CAN SEE THEIR
BREATH
LOVED ONES &
SAY ADIDS
ADIOS & YOU
WAIT FOR THE
LAST
11/26/20

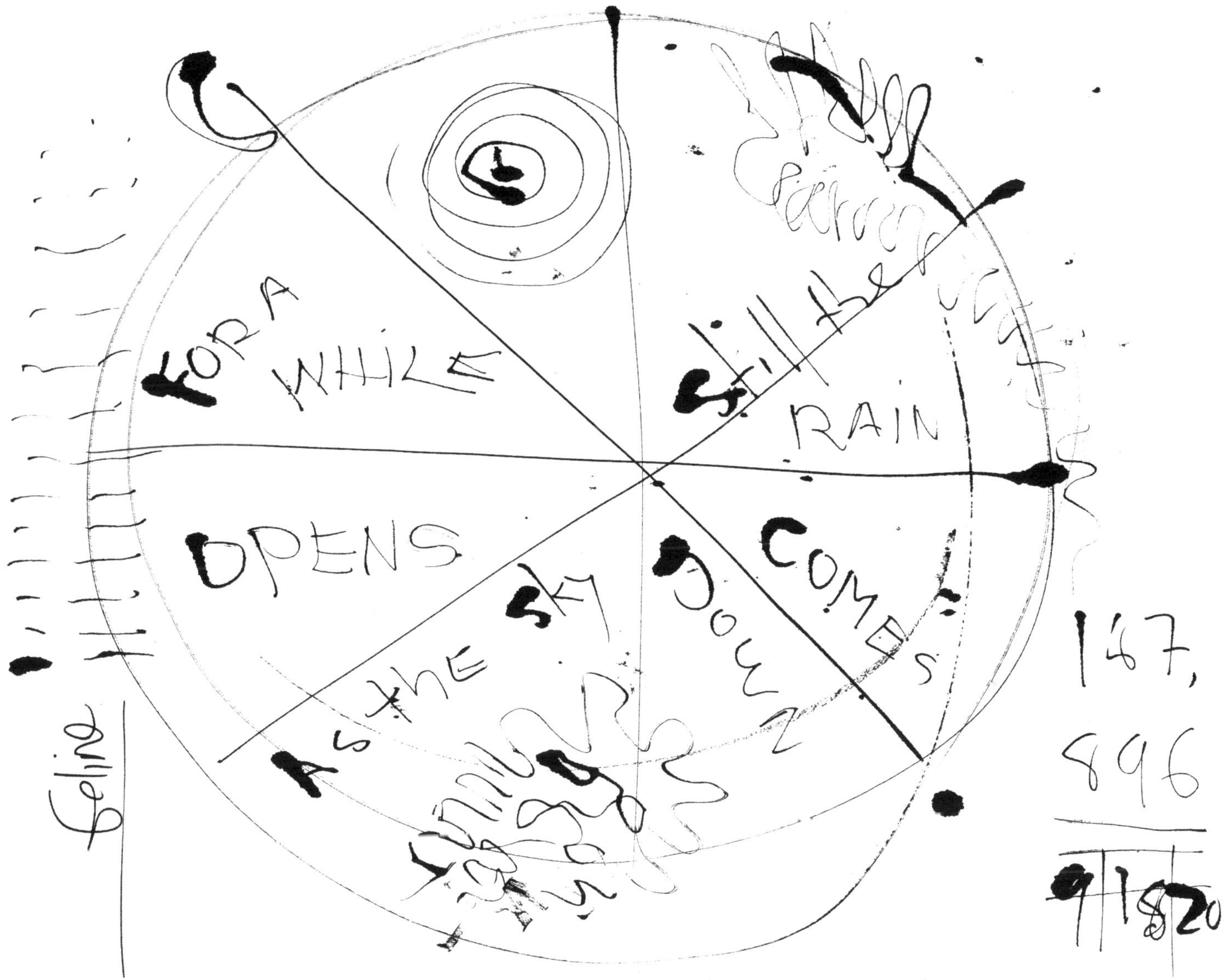

For a
WHILE
still the
RAIN
COMES
DOWN
As the SKY
OPENS
feline
147,
896
9 18 20

MEDITATION III

ALL OF US

i howl like a wolf

great mama Juana
satellites and a photo of our poem

move love
see the way it is all we have
for a while

still
the rain comes
thru the explosions entangled stars

peace

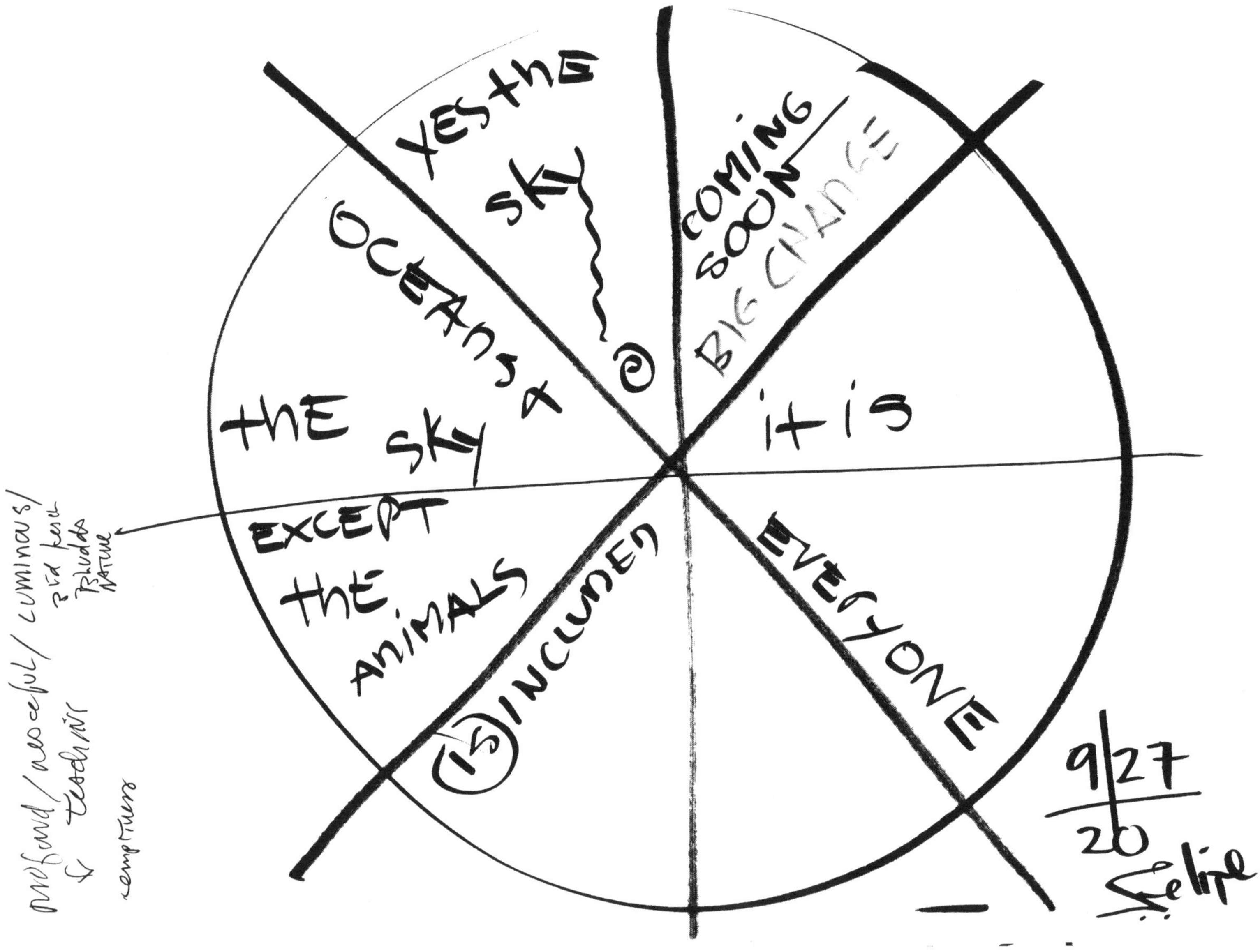
yes the sky
oceans & the sky
coming soon
BIG CHANGE
it is
everyone
(is) included
except the animals
9/27/20
Felipe

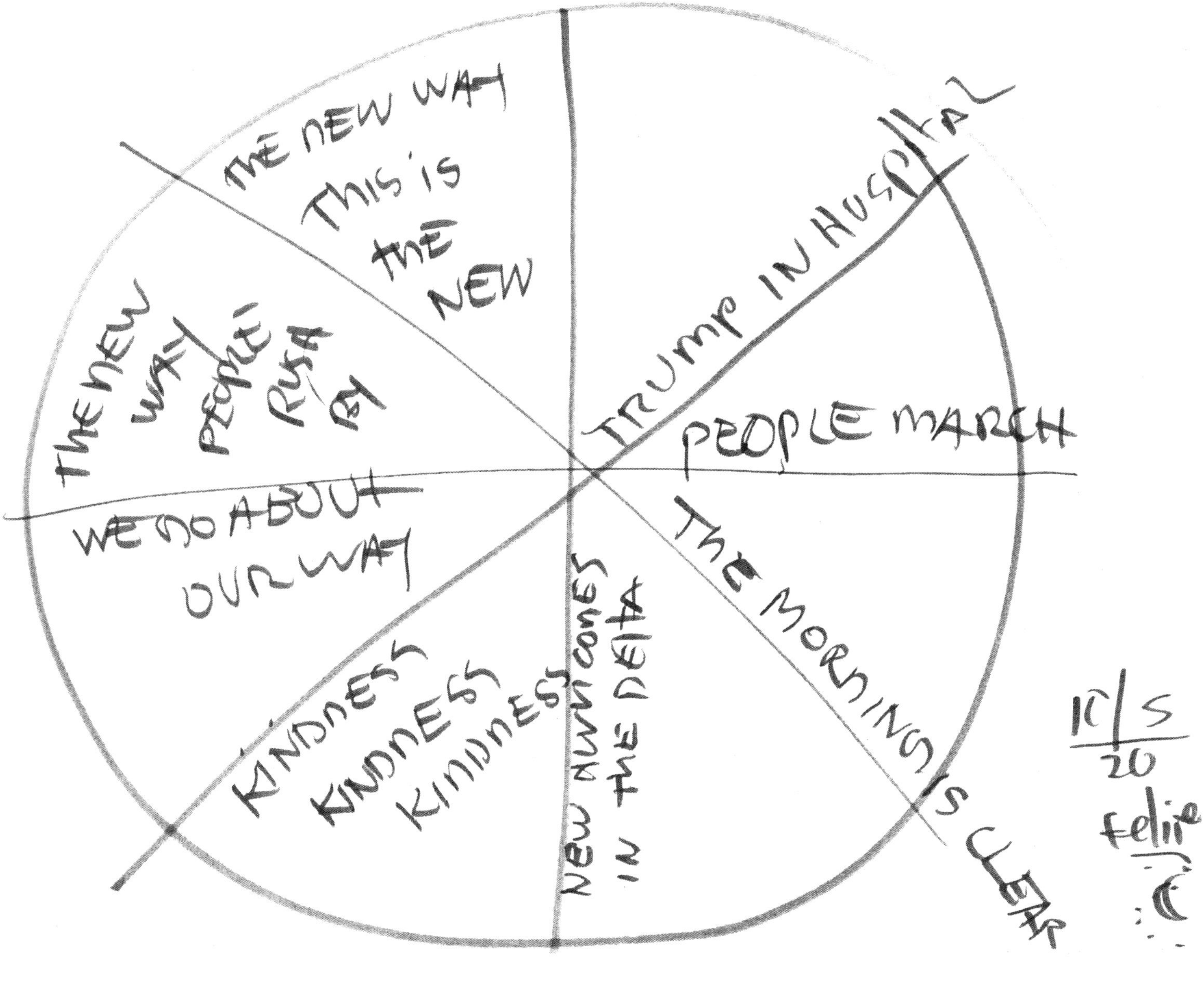
THE NEW WAY
THIS IS THE NEW
TRUMP IN HOSPITAL
PEOPLE MARCH
THE MORNING IS CLEAR
NEW NEWS COMES IN THE DELTA
KINDNESS
KINDNESS
KINDNESS
WE GO ABOUT OUR WAY
10/5/20

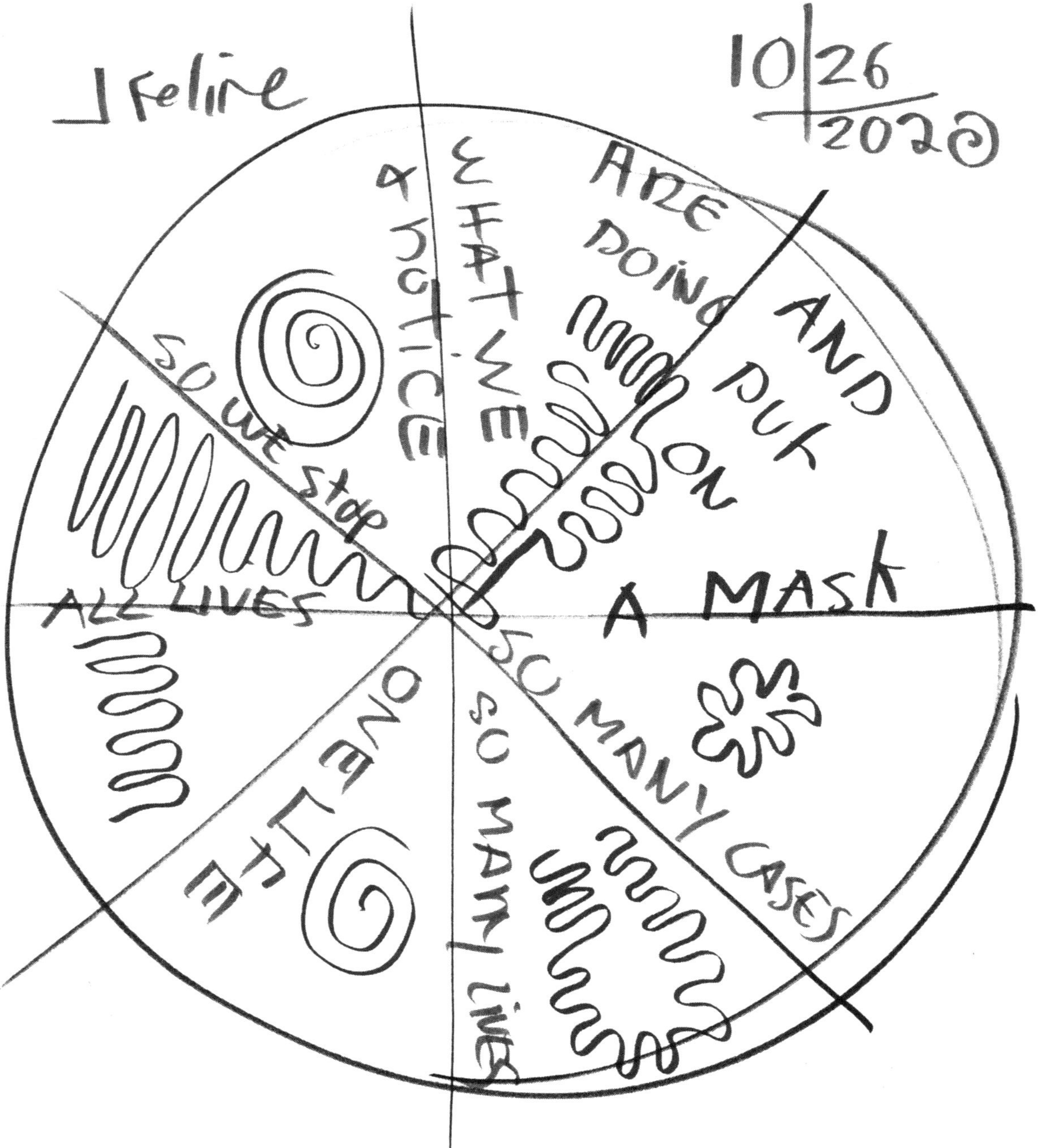

J Feline
10/26/2020
SO WE STOP
& NOTICE
WHAT WE
ARE DOING
AND PUT
ON
A MASK
SO MANY CASES
SO MANY LIVES
ONE LIFE
ALL LIVES

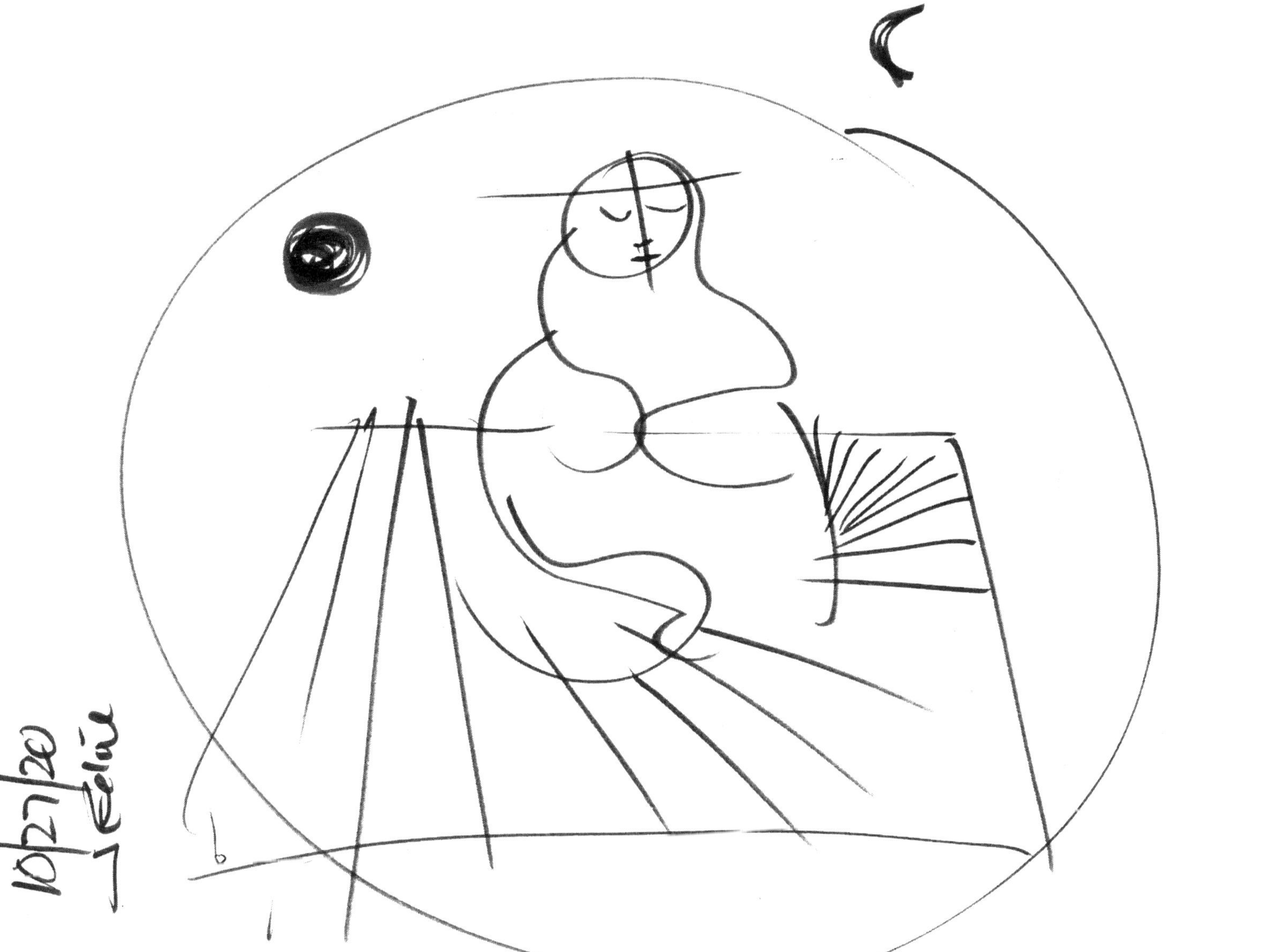

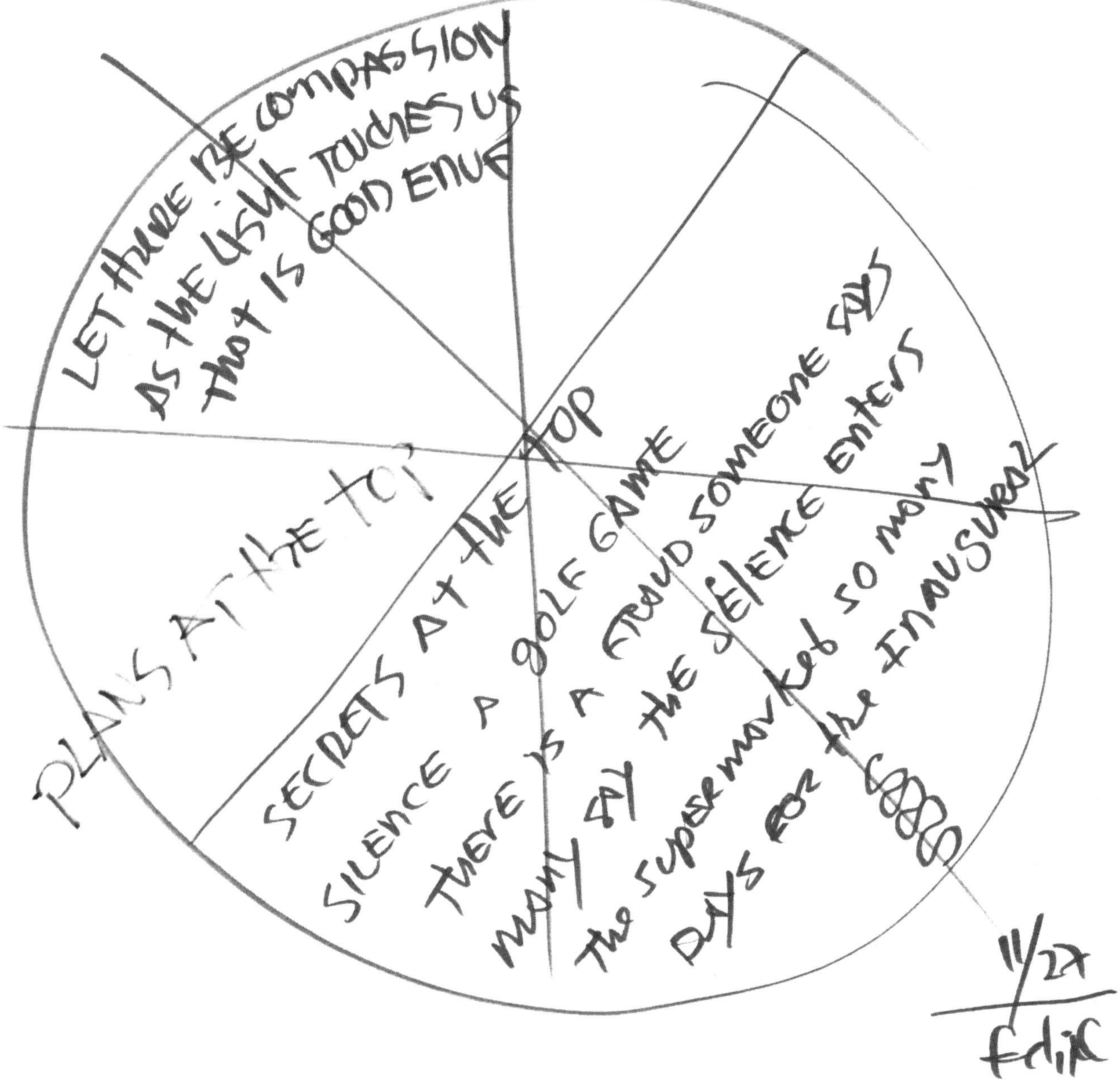
LET THERE BE COMPASSION
AS THE LIGHT TOUCHES US
THAT IS GOOD ENUF
PLANS AT THE TOP
SECRETS AT THE TOP
SILENCE A GOLF GAME
THERE IS A FRAUD SOMEONE SAYS
MANY SAY THE SILENCE ENTERS
THE SUPERMARKET SO MANY
DAYS FOR THE INAUGURAL
11/27
felix

COSMIC
PACHAMAMA
SACRED
FLORES
GRANADA
OJOS CAFES
PAPER CLIP
STREAM
TERRA
RIVER
BIG FULL BELLY WARRIOR
OPEN
STARS
SUNSET
FIRE SIDE
CHOCOLATE

THERE IS A POEM
IN HERE

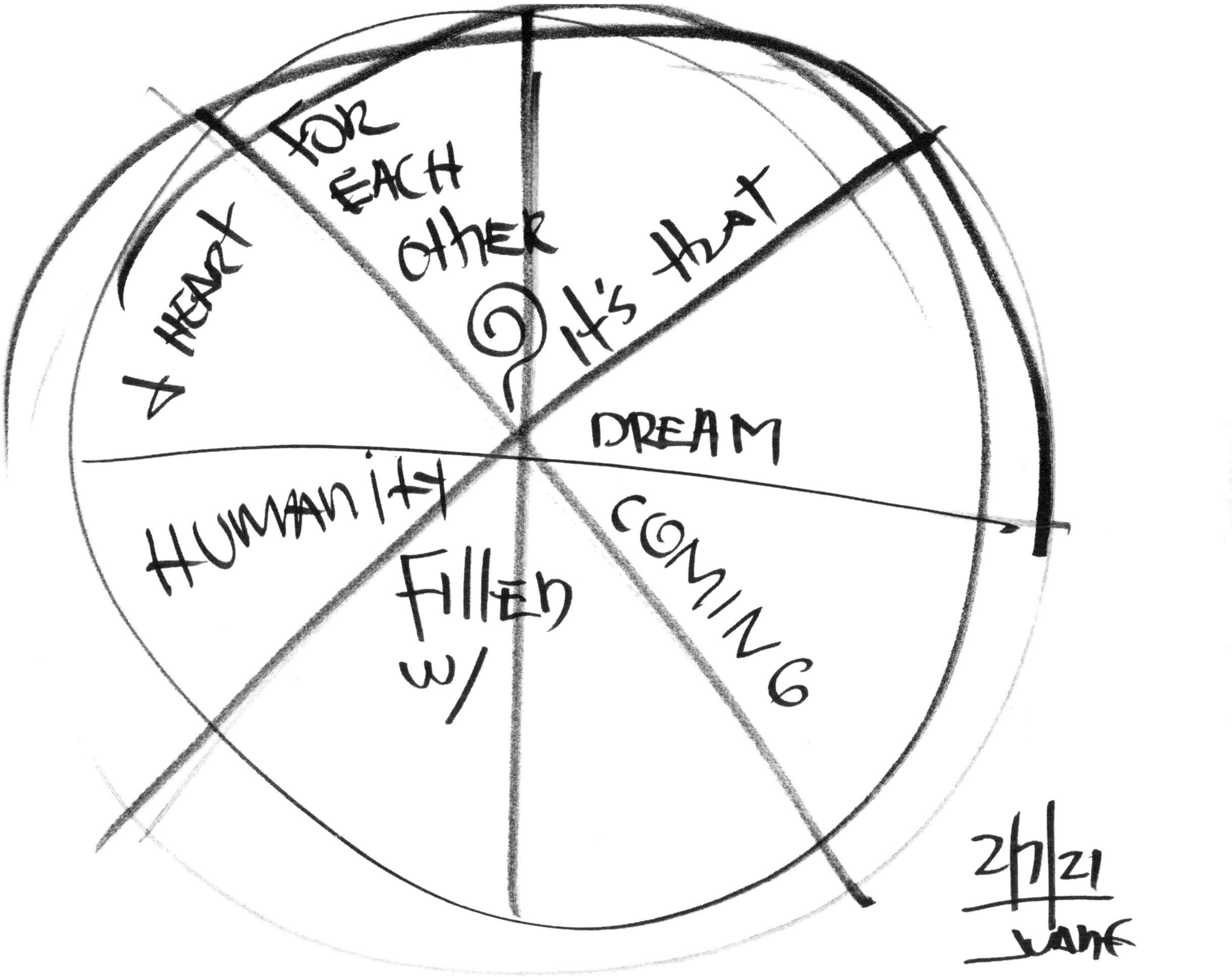
A HEART
FOR EACH OTHER
It's that
DREAM
COMING
HUMANity
Filled
w/
2/7/21

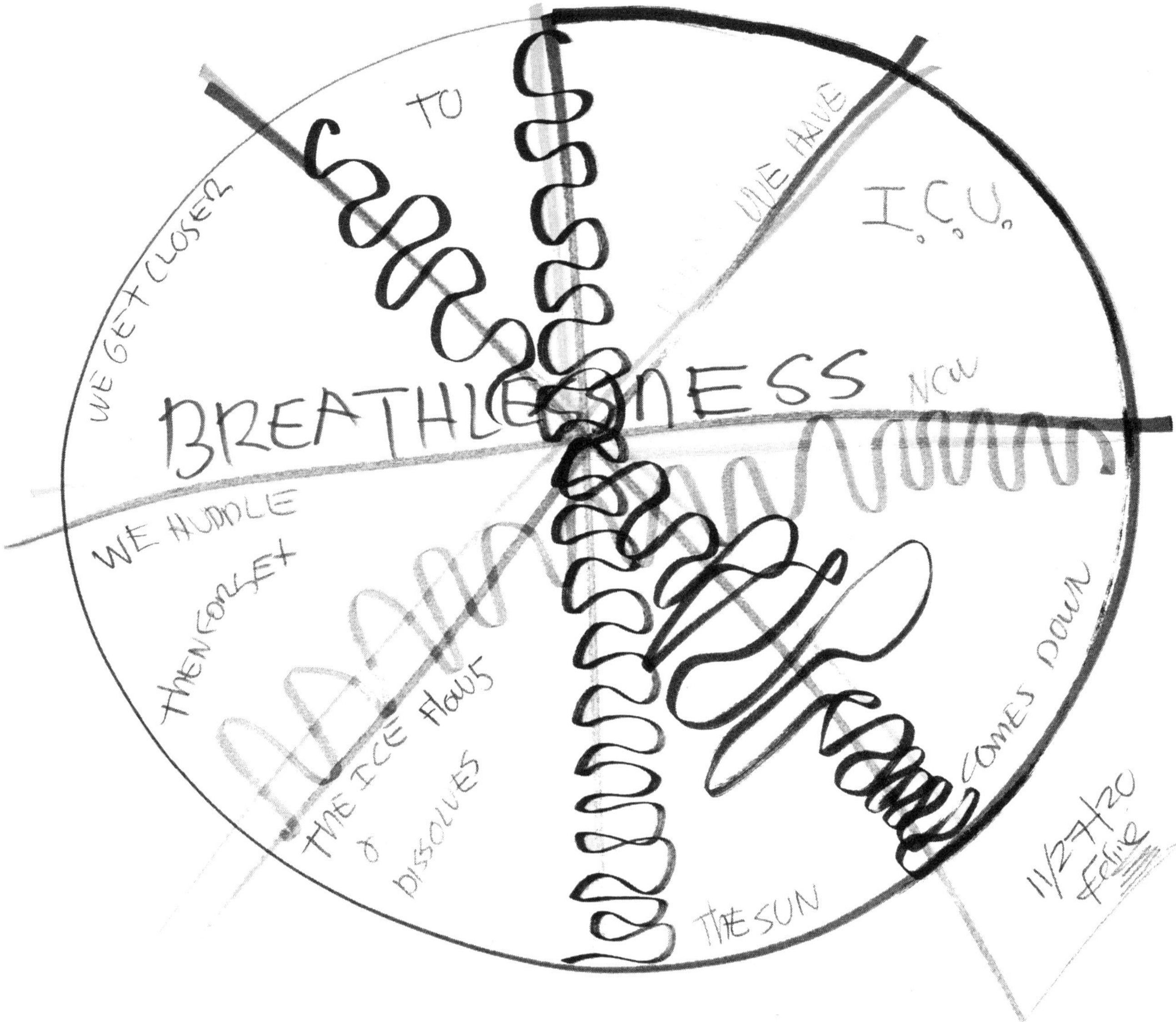
BREATHLESSNESS
WE GET CLOSER
TO
WE HAVE
I.C.U.
NOW
COMES DOWN
THE SUN
THE ICE FLOWS
&
DISSOLVES
THEN FORGET
WE HUDDLE
11/27/20

SUN
POEMS
IN THE WINTER
11/20/20

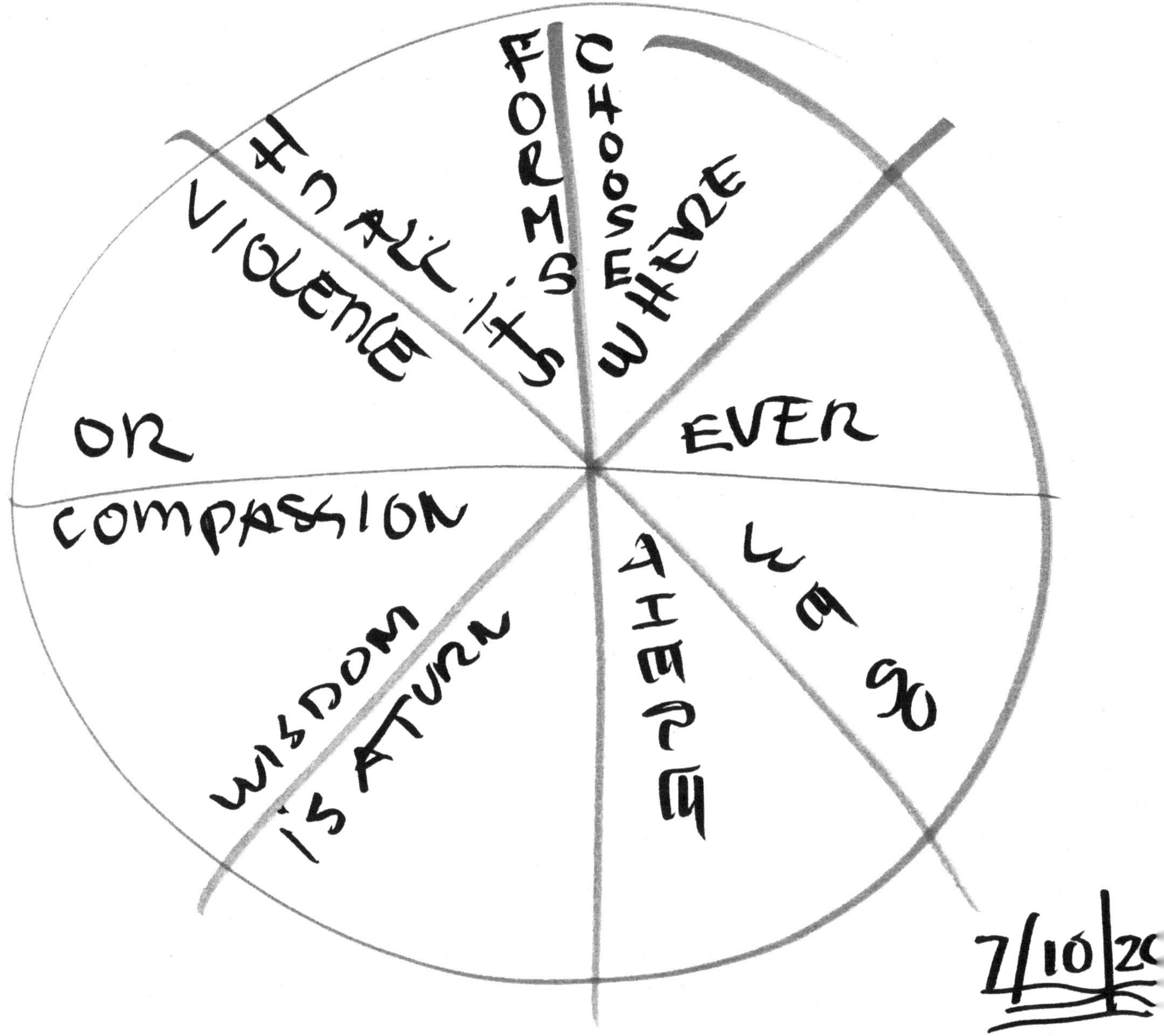

WISDOM
IS A TURN
THERE
WE GO
EVER
WHERE
CHOOSE
FORMS
ITS ALL
VIOLENCE
OR
COMPASSION
7/10/20

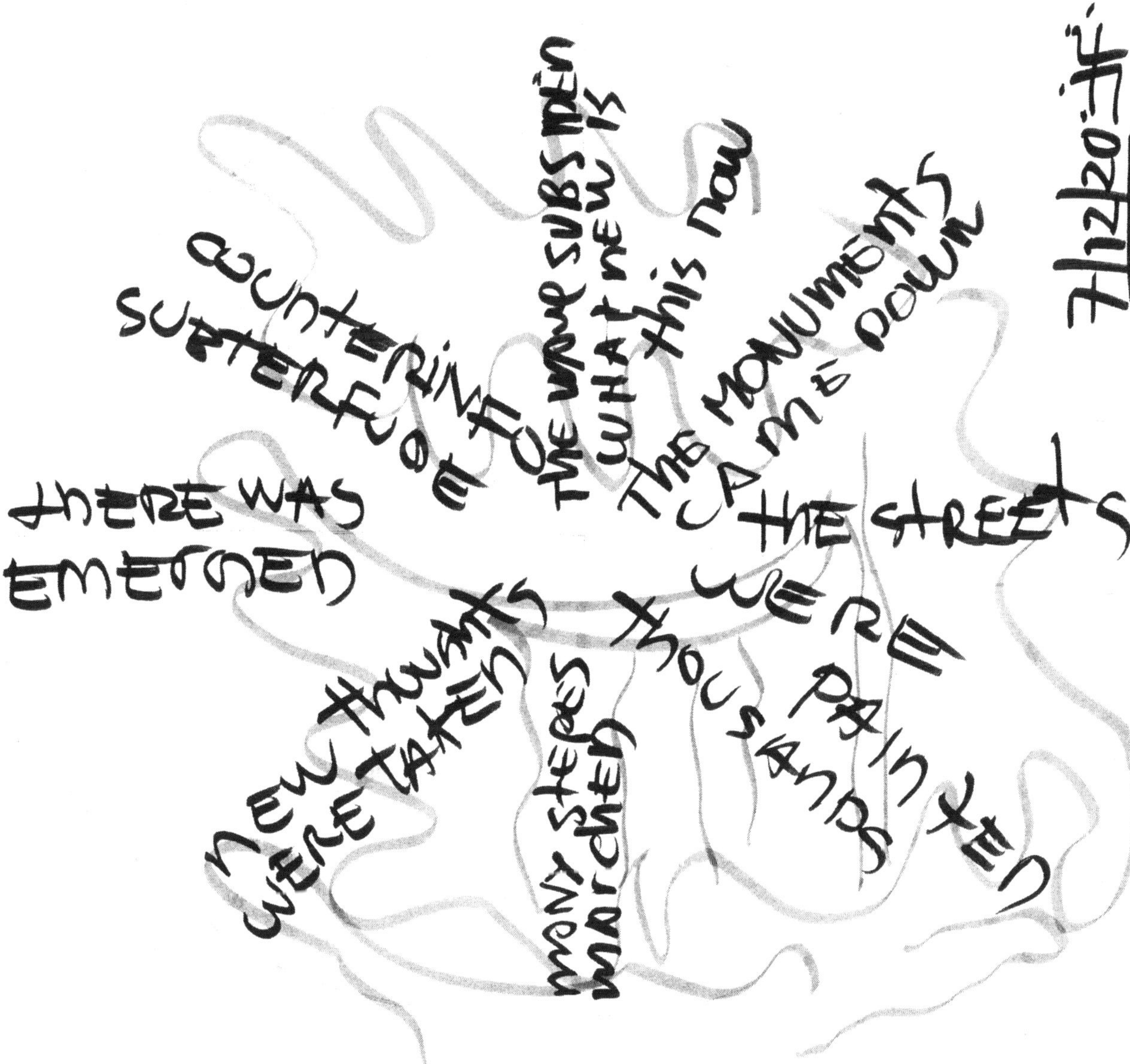
THERE WAS
EMERGED
SUBTERFUGE
WHAT NEW IS
THIS NOW
THE MONUMENTS
CAME DOWN
THE STREETS
WERE PAINTED
THOUSANDS
MANY STEPS
MARCHED
NEW THOUGHTS
WERE TAKEN

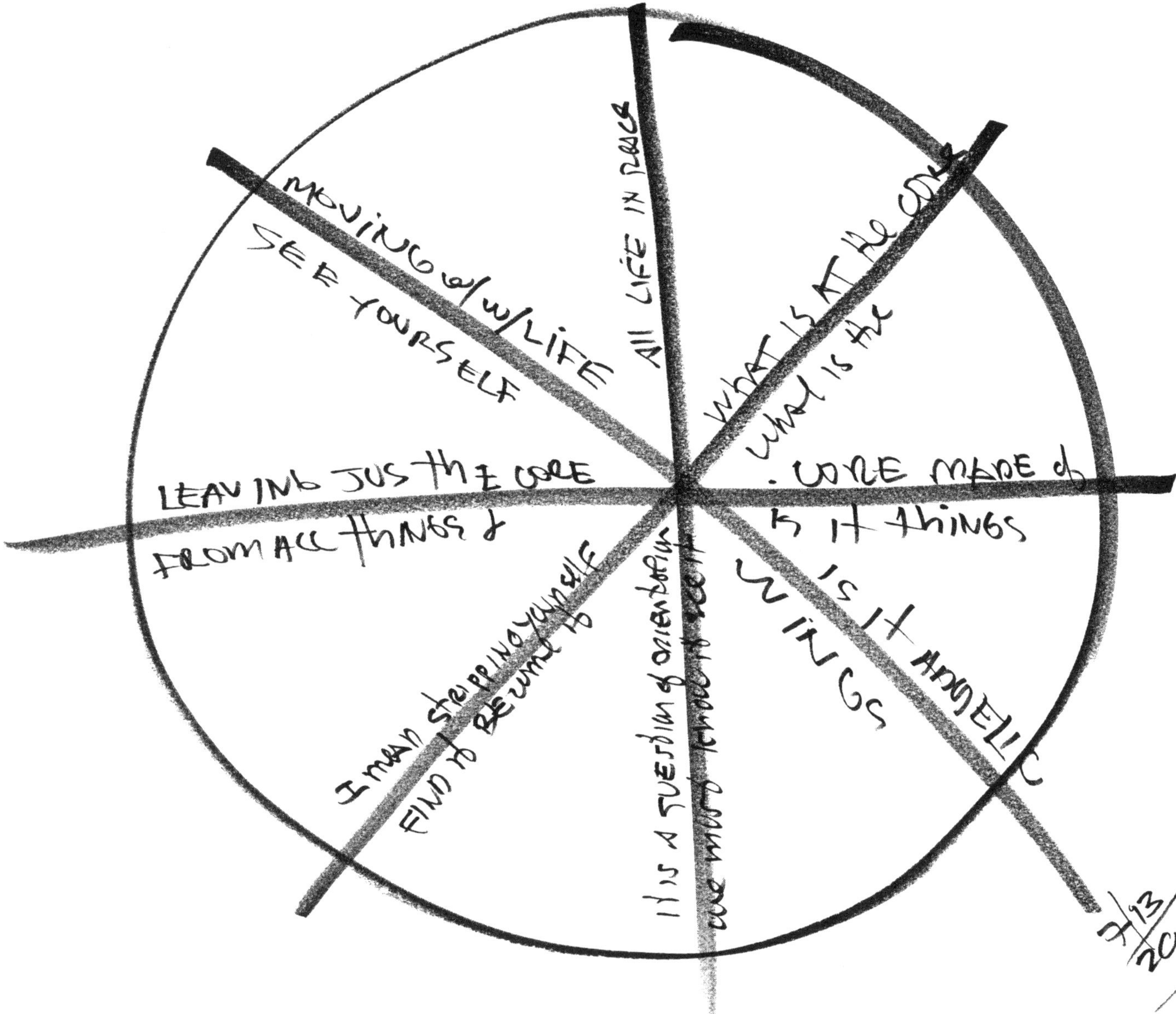
MOVING w/ w/ LIFE
SEE YOURSELF
ALL LIFE IN PEACE
WHAT IS AT THE CORE
what is the
CORE MADE of
IS IT THINGS
IS IT ANGELIC
WINGS
LEAVING JUST THE CORE
FROM ALL THINGS &
I mean stripping yourself
IT IS A QUESTION of ORIENTATION
7/13/20. JF.

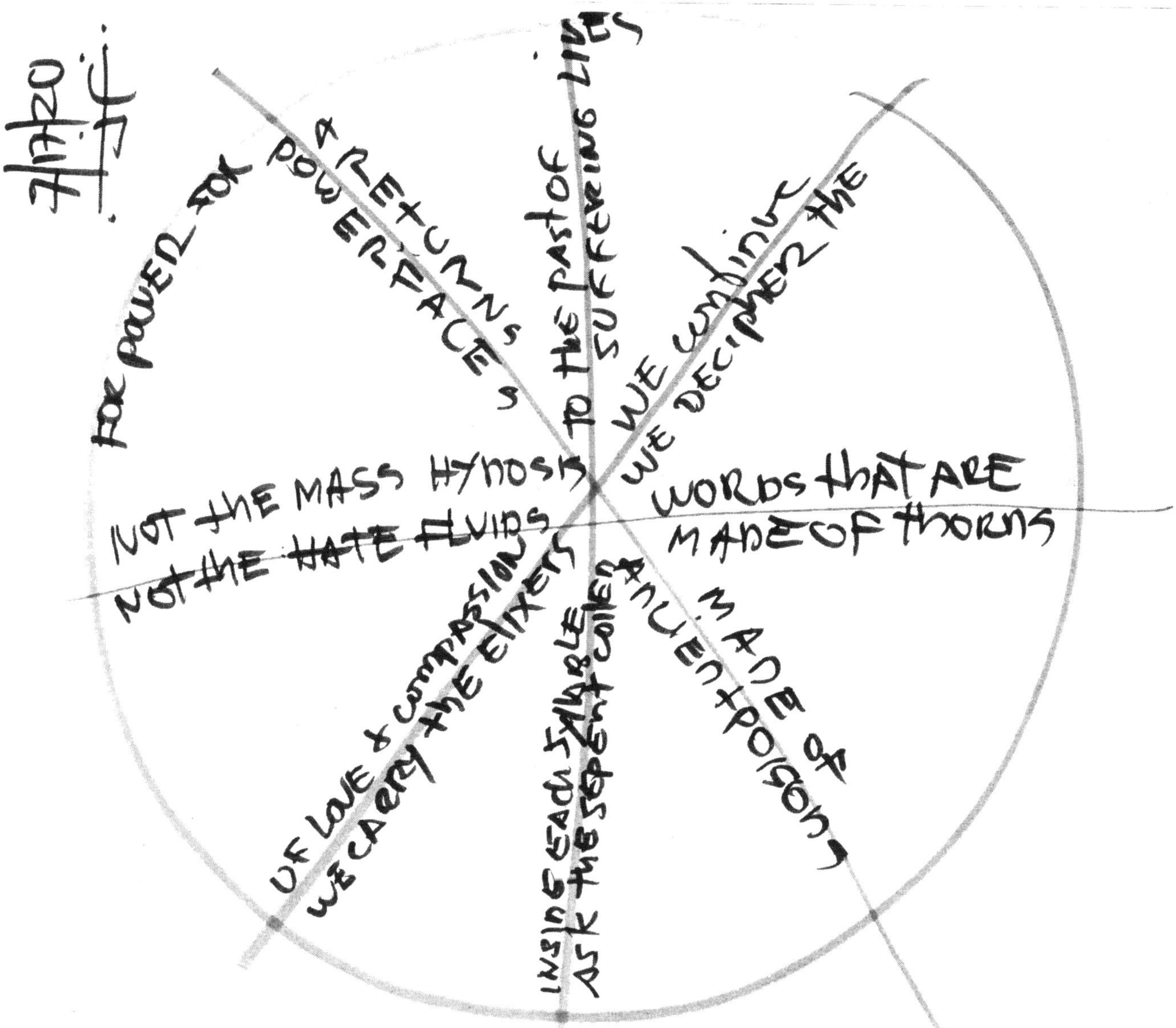

FOR POWER FOR A RETURNS
POWER FACES
TO THE PAST OF LIVES
SUFFERING
WE CONTINUE
WE DECIPHER THE
WORDS THAT ARE
MADE OF THORNS
MADE OF
ANCIENT POISON
INSIDE EACH SYLLABLE
ASK THE SERPENT COILED
OF LOVE & COMPASSION
WE CARRY THE ELIXERS
NOT THE MASS HYPNOSIS
NOT THE HATE FLUIDS

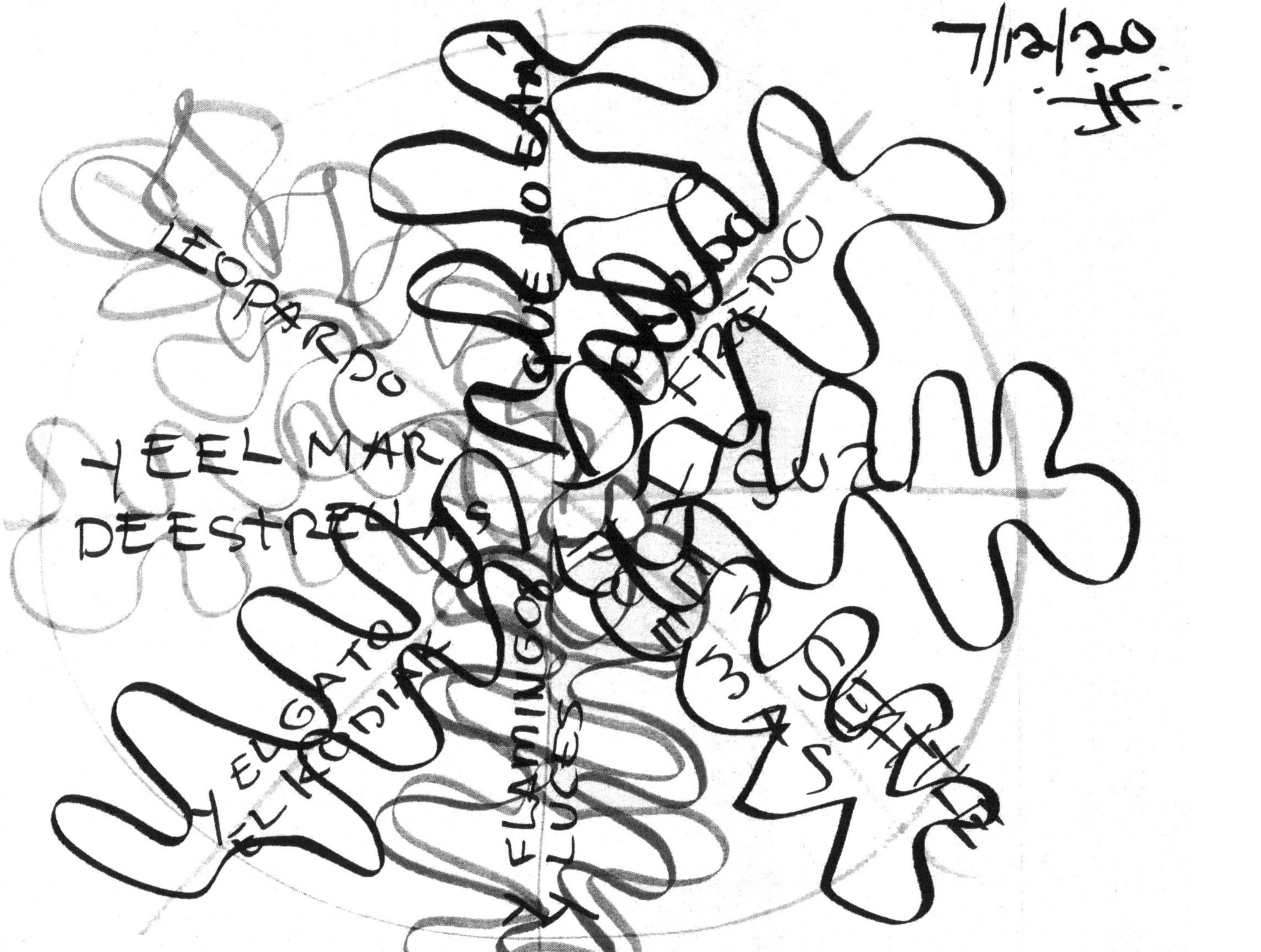
7/12/20
LEOPARDO
Y EL MAR
DE ESTRELLAS
EL GATO
FLAMINGO
LUCES
FREDO

WE WALK FORWARD W/ EACH OTHER
POWER PINNACLE
FROM THE
POWER PINNACLE
THERE IS DENIAL
WE NOTICE THE
WE SEE YOU
WE SCRABBLE
BELOW WE
WE SEE MOST OF ALL
THEN WE WONDER

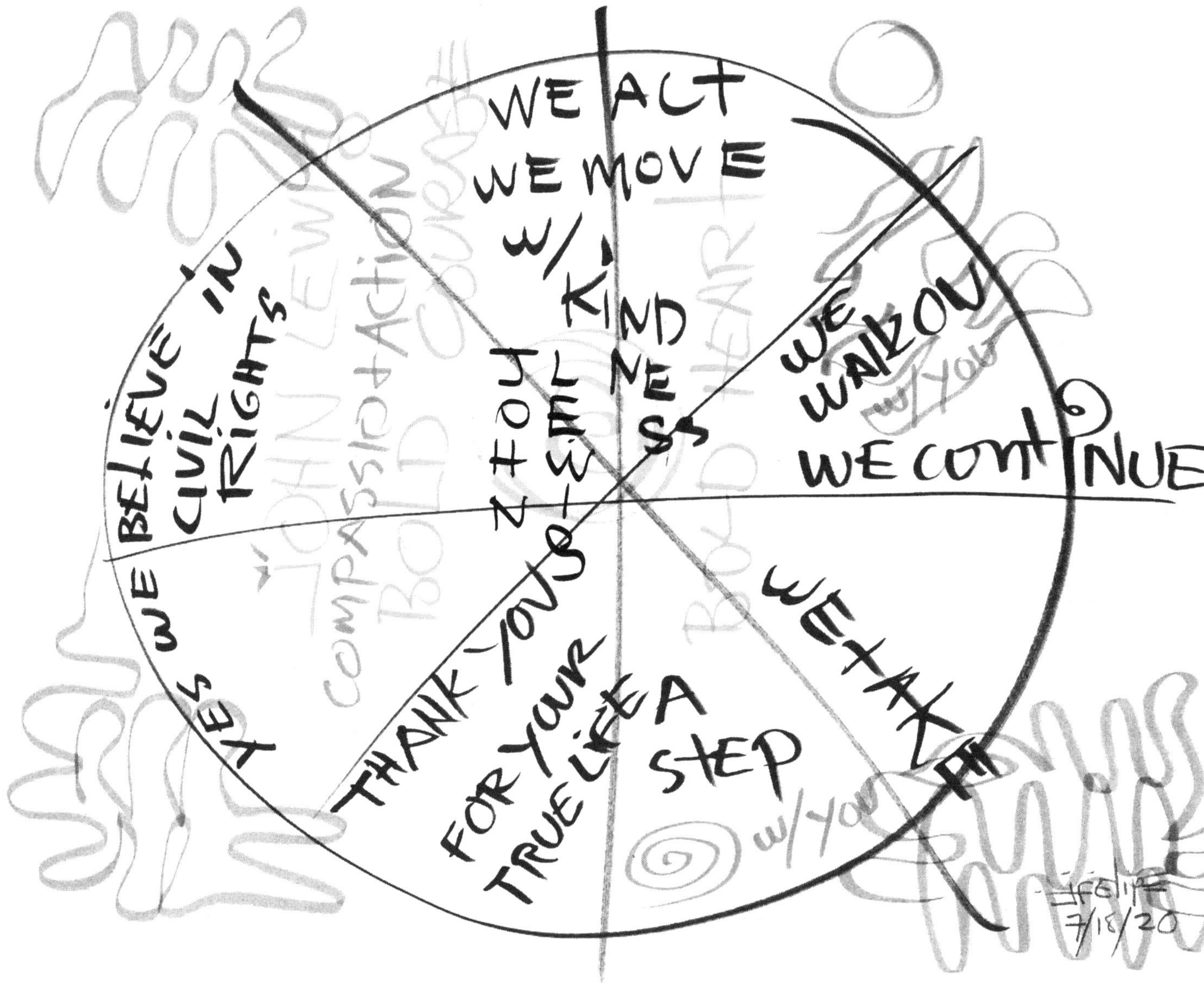
WE ACT
WE MOVE
W/ KINDNESS
YES WE BELIEVE IN CIVIL RIGHTS
JOHN LEWIS
COMPASSION + ACTION
BOLD
WE WALK W/ YOU
WE CONTINUE
WE TAKE
A STEP
W/ YOU
THANK YOU FOR YOUR TRUE LIFE
7/18/20

UNENDING
MAY KINDNESS
OVERFLOW
FROM EVERY
HEART
& HOUSE
& THE
FOUNTAIN
OF ALL
OUR LIVES
ONE
FOUNTAIN
7/22/20

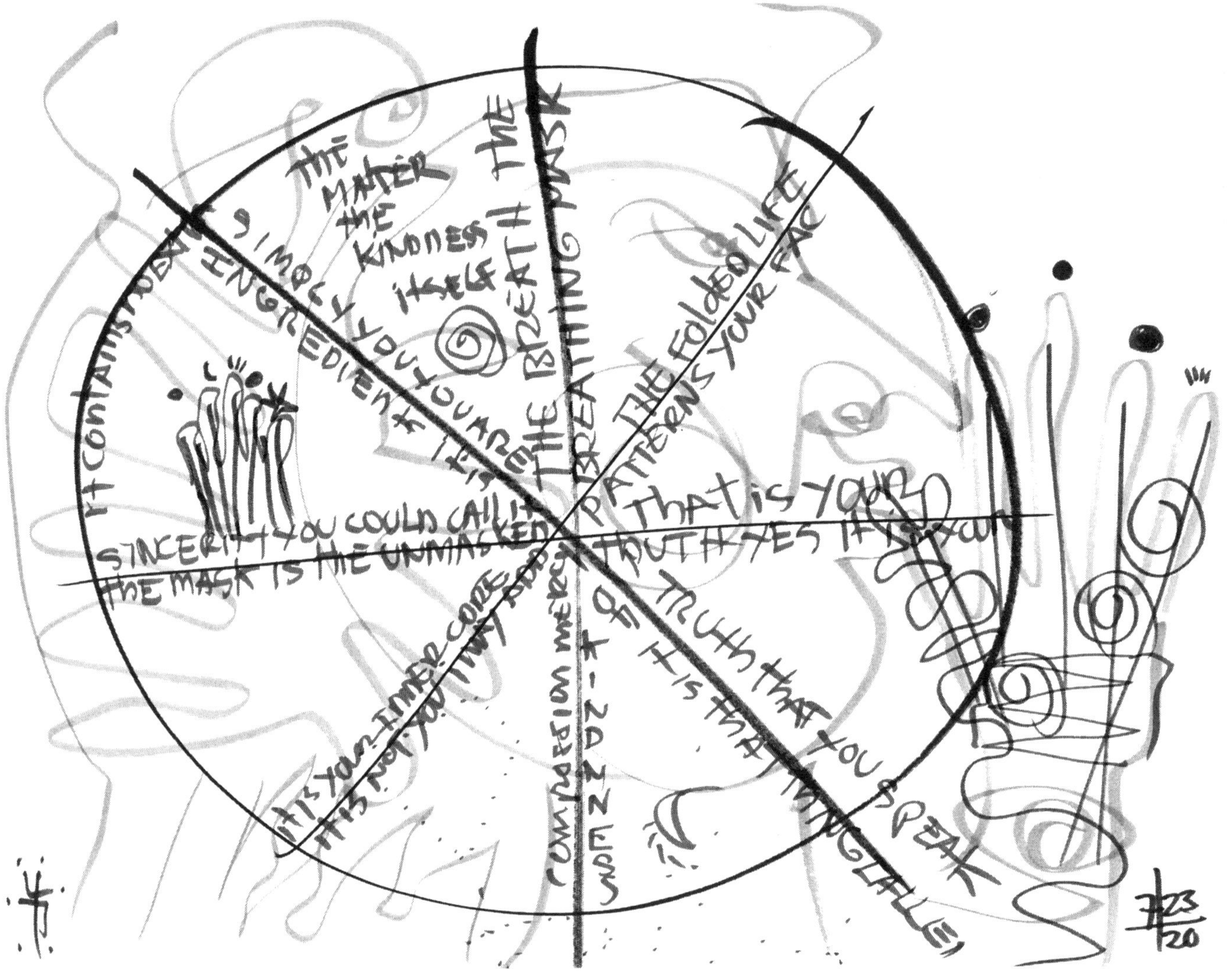

THE MATTER THE KINDNESS ITSELF
THE BREATH THE BREATHING MASK
THE FOLDED LIFE PATTERNS YOUR FAC
THAT IS YOUR TRUTH YES IT IS YOUR
SINCERITY YOU COULD CALL IT
THE MASK IS THE UNMASKED
OF TRUTH THAT YOU SPEAK

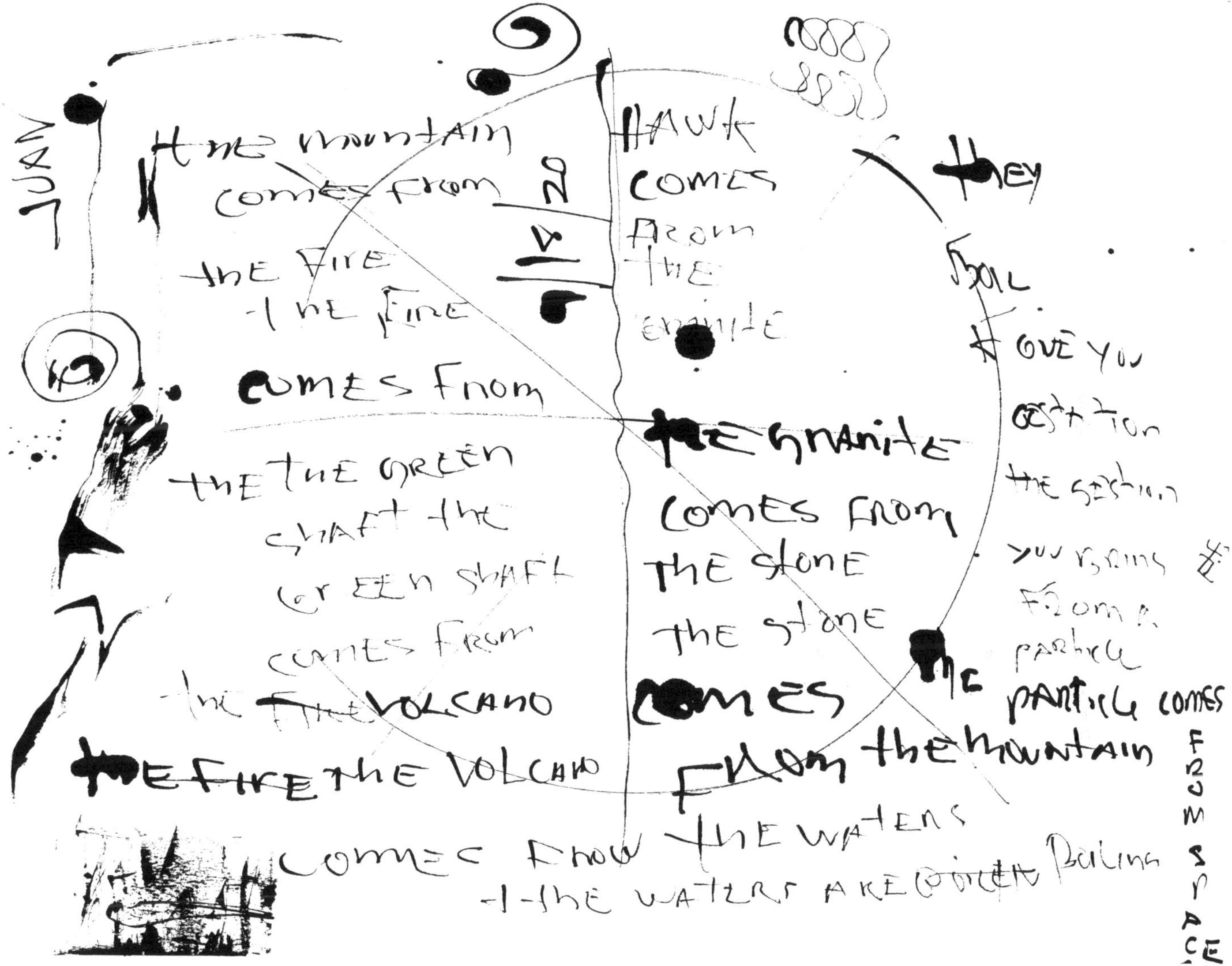

JUAN
the mountain
comes from
the fire
the fire
comes from
the the green
shaft the
green shaft
comes from
the fire VOLCANO
the fire the volcano
comes from the waters
the waters are
hawk
comes
from
the
granite
the granite
comes from
the stone
the stone
comes
from the mountain
they
soil
love you
gestation
the gestation
you brains
from a
particle
the particle comes
from space
Boiling

GARDENS OF PEACE
THAT UNITE
ALL OF US
+ IS THE STILLNESS THE
SO WE BREATHE
SO WE MARCH
QUIET & STILL
TALL & LOUD THEN
THRU FLAMES NIGHT
SO WE BREATHE
TEAR
THROUGH SMOKE & TEAR GAS

DE VIDAS
DE MILES
UN COLOR
DE MIL COLORES
ALFREDO
UNA VIDA
UN DANZÓN
UNA
CANCION
UNAS MARACAS
UN TAMBOR
UN LIMÓN
UNA GUITARRA

MEDITATION IV

NOTHING CHANGES EVEN WHEN IT CHANGES

kindness
cosmos
kindness
cosmos

::

un nuevo día

::

today the
sun and the geraniums
the leaves trees
birds
see it everywhere

::

cosmic flow ocean wind earth space
cosmic flow

::

flow

::

do not think
we are all in different places
the war has opened us all

::

we are face to face &
far away

::

there are missiles coming down &

bombs coming down
you can see them
in the night flowering
red orange fierce lamps

::

it is another world unfolding
it has no name

::

its goal is to erase all the names
yours in particular mine in particular
all of our names

::

dreams of fire only fire

& rubble
& stones
& splinters
& metal sheets of T-72 battle tanks

::

everyone is thirsty
everyone is freezing
everyone searches for bread & dreams of milk &
a hammer to rebuild

::

nothing changes
even when it changes

::

a handful of gravel
a handful of Ukraine

a tiny daughter says
reaching Poland
never forget

:::

a mother and her two children
escape the city toward
freedom—
the mortars cut them &
burn their flesh yet they
breathe & their bicycle & tires still spin
under the expanse of the scalded skies

::

all is flow all is cosmos & gravel

all is in movement and rotation

all is kindness & peace without war

all lives
all lives
all lives
all life
                                        is one

THIS IS HOW WE HEAL
WORDS FROM
HEART GIVING
ALL
IS
TODAY
THE HEART
LIFE GIVING

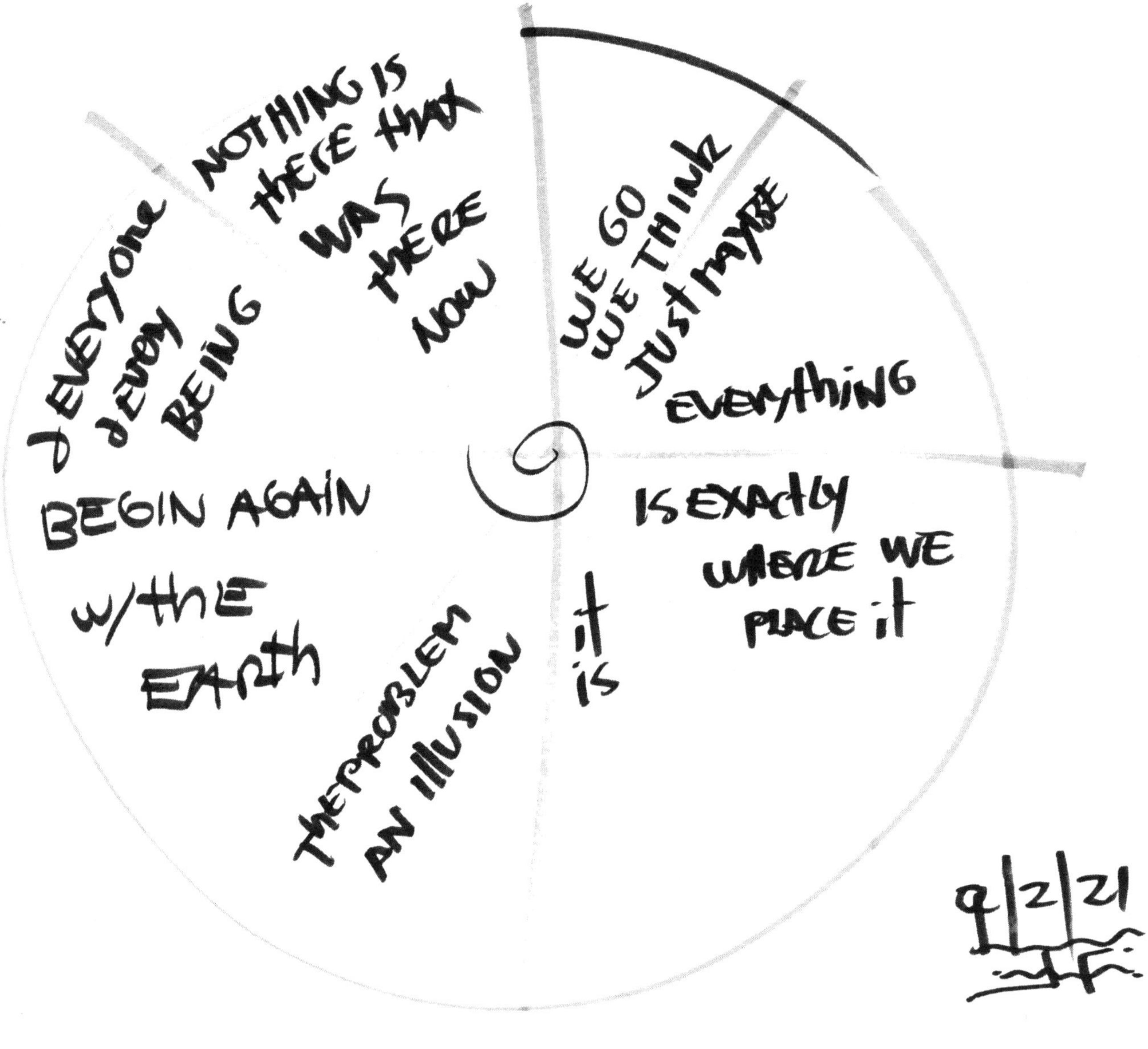
NOTHING IS
THERE THAT
WAS
THERE
NOW
& EVERYONE
& EVERY
BEING
WE GO
WE THINK
JUST MAYBE
EVERYTHING
IS EXACTLY
WHERE WE
PLACE IT
BEGIN AGAIN
W/THE
EARTH
THE PROBLEM
AN ILLUSION
IT
IS
9/2/21

Blasts heard in multiple cities blasts in the shape of stars no one knows no one expected where
why? why? why?
so we go
& we walk
where
why
we sit in a circle with our bodies shielding Ukraine our land

TEN DAYS AGO
YOU WERE A TEACHER
Accountant Journalist
DANCER
THERE IS HOPE ONLY
THERE IS COURAGE ONLY
there is unity now

HERE YOU ARE IN POLAND SIGN IN

I ASKED my DAUGHTER "what's THAT IN YOUR HAND it's GRAVEL isn't it?"
"YES, SHE SAID.."
"why.."
"SO I WONT FORGET my COUNTRY. SO I WONT FORGET my UKRAINE."

WITH DAUGHTERS
AND SONS
SANDBAGS ONE BY ONE
HOLOCAUST SURVIVORS
BEGIN AGAIN

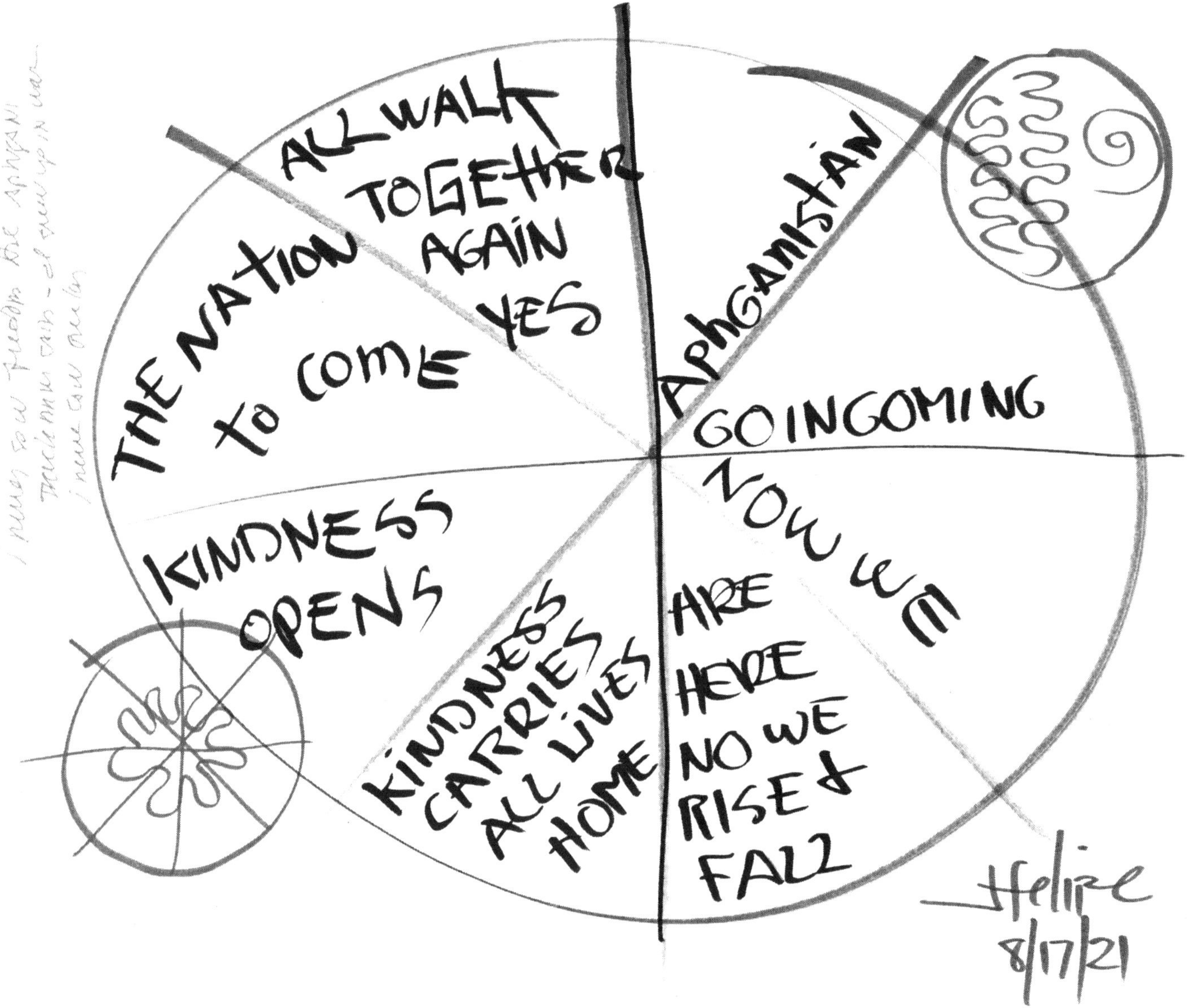
ALL WALK
TOGETHER
AGAIN
YES
THE NATION
to COME
Aphganistan
GOINGOMING
NOW WE
ARE
HERE
NO WE
RISE &
FALL
KINDNESS
OPENS
KINDNESS
CARRIES
ALL LIVES
HOME
Jfelipe
8/17/21

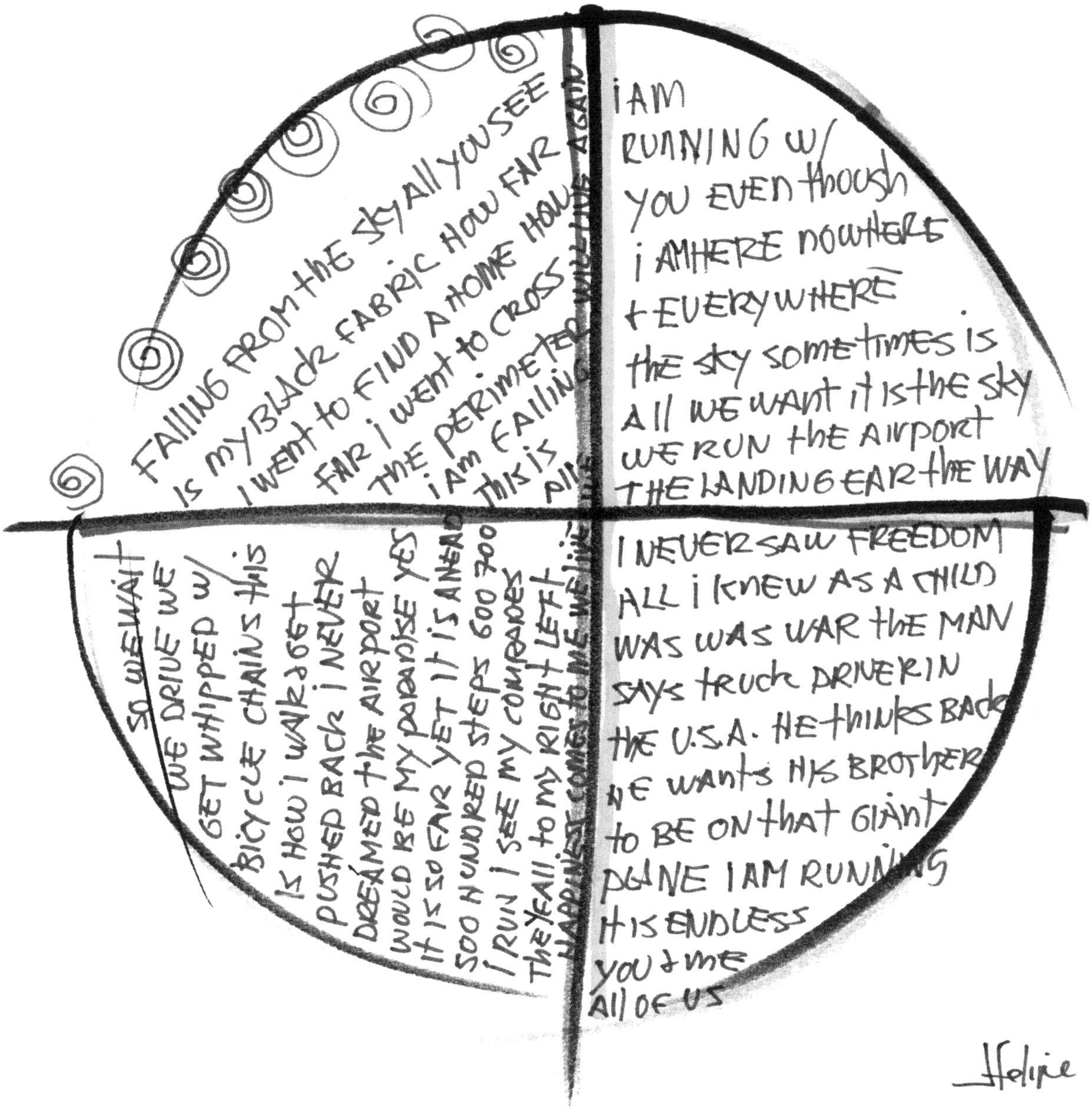

Felipe 8/18/21

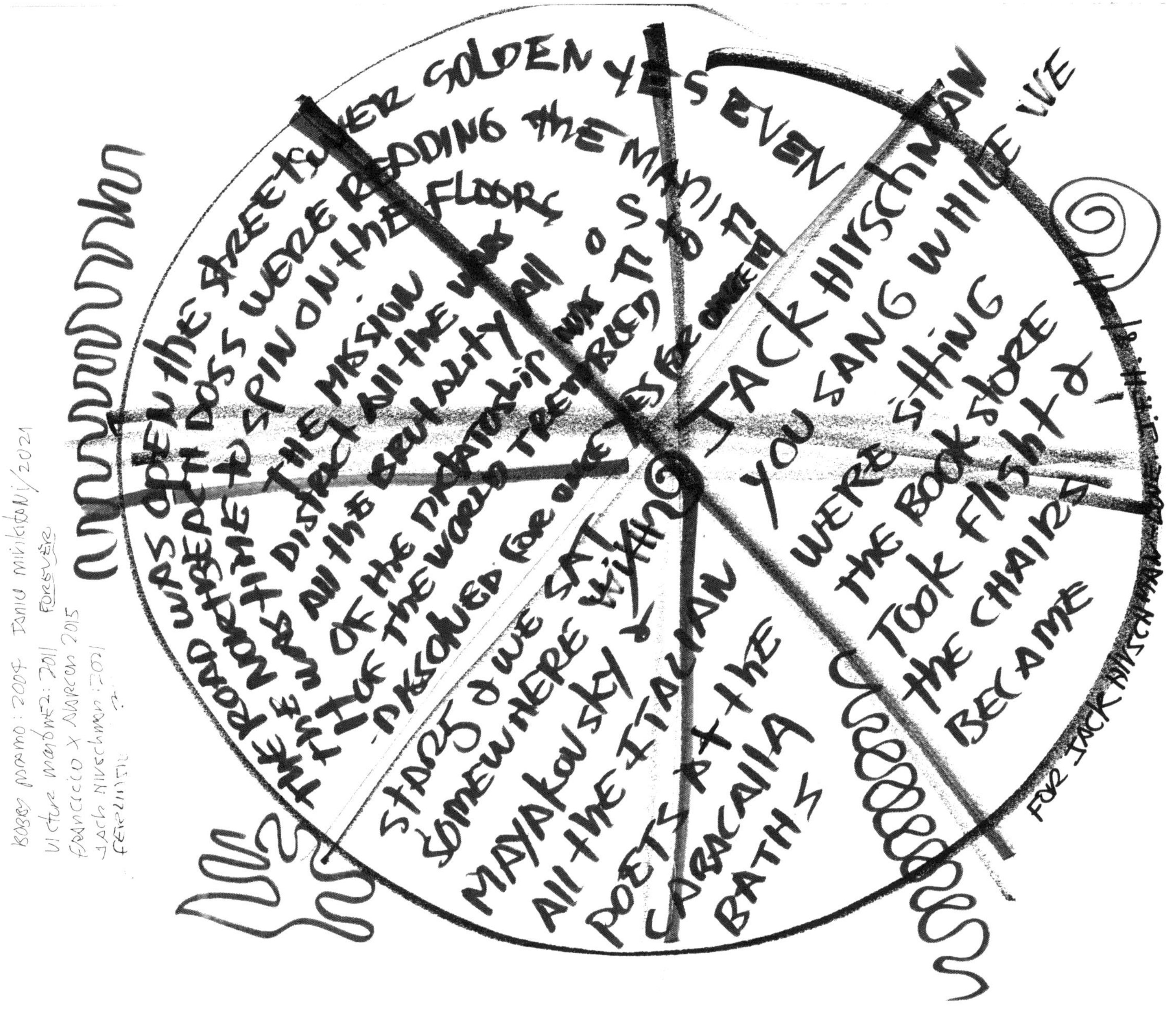
THE ROAD WAS OPEN THE STREETS WER GOLDEN YES EVEN
JACK HIRSCHMAN
YOU SANG WHILE WE
WERE SITTING
THE BOOKSTORE
TOOK FLIGHT &
THE CHAIRS
BECAME
STARS & WE SAT
SOMEWHERE WITH
MAYAKOVSKY &
ALL THE ITALIAN
POETS AT THE
CARACALLA
BATHS
FOR JACK HIRSCHMAN
Victor Martinez: 2011
Francisco X Alarcon 2015
Jack Hirschman: 2021
FOREVER

THERE'S MORE YOU
ARE the EMERGENCY
EMERGENCY
EVERYWHERE!
FOOD WATER CLOTHES HOUSE STREET
WOMENS RIGHTS
DID YOU NOTICE ?
FLOODS WARS DIVISIONS

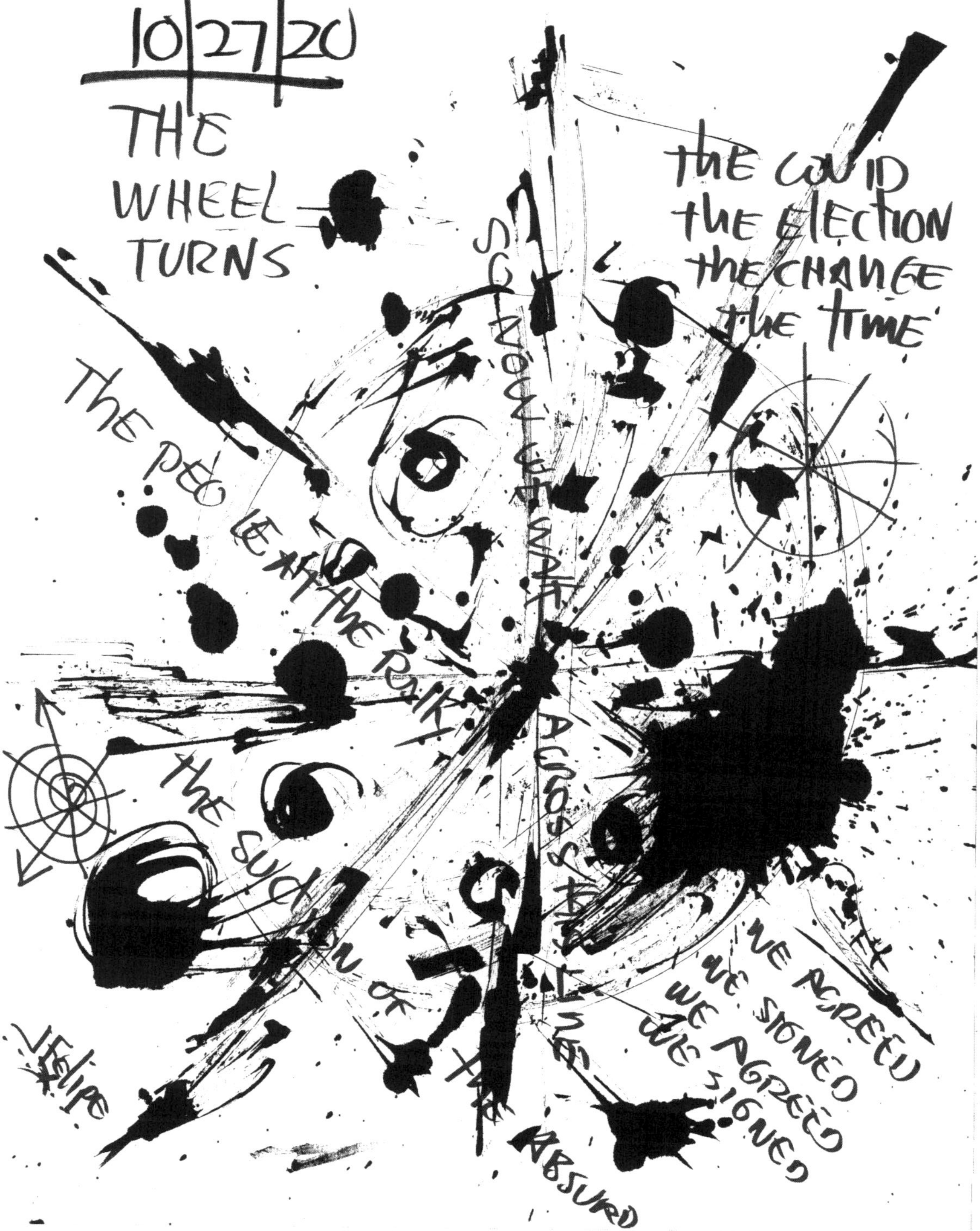
10/27/20
THE WHEEL TURNS
THE COVID
THE ELECTION
THE CHANGE
THE TIME
WE AGREED
WE SIGNED
WE AGREED
WE SIGNED
THE SUCTION OF THE ABSURD
J.Felipe

the mountain
notices
this
now
do you
see
it
we wait
it seems
for the
dawn
we forget
we
are
the
dawn
we forget the
the dawn
is made of
light
we forget
the light
is written
on our
face
9/1/21

ACKNOWLEDGMENTS

Gracias & Love, Always:

For Margo & all our familias, for my children and grandchildren, great grandchildren—and my mother, Lucha and father, Felipe & grandparents and great grandparents from long ago. Gracias to familias de Mesa, AZ, Mesquite, NM, Long Beach, CA & El Paso, TX.

For my cousins, sobrinas and sobrinos, all my familias.

For all my dear friends and students and teachers that have helped and encouraged me along the way.

For Mrs. Lelya Sampson, 103 years old, that has guided me with her heart-words since 3rd grade. I bow to you.

For Fresno State President Dr. Saúl Jimenez-Sandoval for always being most supportive and for providing assistance for our Laureate Lab Visual Wordist Studio at Fresno State—as well as Dr. Joseph Castro and Dr. Lynette Zelezny who were the instrumental in helping me grow the Laureate Lab.

For the Library of Congress, and the late Dr. James Billington, who called on me to be the Poet Laureate of the USA in 2015, as well as Robert Casper of the Poetry and Literary Division of the Library that inspired me and led me through the steps. I also thank Dr. Carla Hayden that believed in me.

I thank all. So many good-hearted teachers, friends, poets, families and you. Gracias to Monarch School, San Diego, CA.

I thank all the schools that invited me to read at their site, and to meet their students, and communities. Also, I thank Kendra Marcus and Minju Chang, my literary agents, that have moved my work forward for decades. Also, I thank Blue Flower Arts, Lecture Agency, for working day and night on my behalf to arrange my travel and invitations across the globe.

Gracias to JFH Elementary School in Fresno, Principal, Miguel Naranjo and Vice Principal, Sarah Chavez for all their inspiration and hard work. As well as all the teachers and their daily creative projects with our beautiful children and parents.

Gracias to Alfredo Arreguín (RIP) and his wife Susan, for lending us his two-story mural for our JFH Elementary school in Fresno, and for the cover art for this collection.

I thank the poets of Fresno, San Francisco, LA, San Diego, the USA and the world for their constant churning of poetry, inspiration, thinking and knowledge and care for the people, its creatures and the earth.

I give many gracias to Anthony Cody for his constant & keen assistance and editing on this collection—as well as Sarah Gzemski and Suzi F. Garcia of Noemi Press.

City Lights Publishing House of San Francisco, Editors, I thank for all the years together—Elaine Katzenberger and Stacey Lewis. Many Gracias.

Most recent, thank you and more gracias to María Maloney of Mouthfeel Press for publishing my recent book, *California Brown.* As well, gracias to FlowerSong Press Publisher, Edward Vidaurre.

And many more years with University of AZ, Tucson Press. Gracias.

I would not have published a word without all of you. And without my dearest poetry/art brothers and sisters now gone: Bobby Paramo, Victor Martinez, Francisco X. Alarcón, Q. R. Hand, Alfonsito Texidor, Jack Hirschman, Al Young, José Montoya, Janice Mirikitani, and Amy Uyematsu.

A shout-out to TZ Hernandez, Carmen Giménez, Lauro Flores, Francisco Lomelí, Rigoberto Gonzalez, Kingfish Alvarez, Bilazo, CPITS, Arlena & Pamilia. Manuel Herrera, Manuel Martin Rodriguez, Paul Flores, Tom Lutz, Josiah Luis Alderete, Deborah Wong, Ginny Lim, Before Columbus Foundation Cadre & again, my children. And, Monarch High School, Logan Heights, San Diego, CA.

For Bob & Rick.

Many thanks to Maceo Montoya and the team at Huizache Magazine for publishing a small collection of The Cosmic Flow Mandalas.

Again:
For Amy Uyematsu, RIP
for my cousins recently gone: Beto, Vicente, Tito & Judy Quintana

Many appreciations to the Barcelona Performance team that took on Manos de Escombros, a poem in performance, regarding the occupation of Ukraine in Spanish.

Many more appreciations for the performance team, the "Quantum Performance Sphere" that took on "Handful of Gravel" regarding the occupation of Ukraine (in English) at UC-Riverside. The UCR project would not have been possible without the Edward A. Dickson Emeritus/a Professorship Award. Gracias to Allison Adelle Hedge Coke and Tom Lutz, the students, and community in Riverside, CA.